PSALMS OF MOTHERHOOD AND OTHER REFLECTIONS ON LIFE

Elizabeth Dettling Moreno

Copyright © 2021 By Elizabeth Dettling Moreno

All rights reserved. Churches and other non-commercial interests may reproduce portions of this book without the express written permission of the author, provided that the text does not exceed five percent of the entire book.

"Scripture taken from the NEW AMERICAN STANDARD BIBLE Copyright 1960, 1962, 1963, 1968, 1971, 1972, 1973, 1975, 1977, 1995 by The Lockman Foundation. Used by permission."

This book was printed in the United States of America.

To order additional copies of this book, contact:

Elizabeth Moreno
Praise77488@sbcglobal.net
Or amazon.com

Opportune Independent Publishing Co.
www.opportunepublishing.com

ISBN: 978-1-0882-3494-5 | Soft-cover | Poetry, Prose And Essays

Dedicated to my Children,
Who gave me the Foundation
For a Work of this Magnitude.

Michael

Patrick

Ada

Chris

Gabriel

Thank you,
my beautiful bunch,
for being part of my journey.
I love you all
more than you can imagine.

Acknowledgments

My heart is full of gratitude to the many people who encouraged me along the way in writing this book. Although these prayer poems were written during the 1970's, the thoughts expressed in them are as true today as they were then. I am so thankful to bring this to completion.

My greatest thanks go to God Himself for guiding me in writing these thoughts and keeping them intact from then until now, about 45 years later. It is my greatest wish for Him to be glorified.

Although my second husband is not now on earth, he goaded me on a regular basis to write this book. He would be so happy to see that it is finally done. Thank you, Baby, for being my cheerleader!

Karen, you have taken his place as my number one encourager. You have managed to criticize with kid gloves and a big dose of love. Thank you for tackling the job with me.

To my son Chris: you delivered me from many technical catastrophes. When I thought all my efforts on the computer had been lost, you worked your magic and resurrected my work. Chris, I could not have done this without you. Thank you!!!

There have been so many people along the way who have given me their encouragement because they love the way I write. Your words of affirmation have kept me going strong. Thank you all from the bottom of my heart.

Photos of Family

The Dettling Siblings 1968

Top Row: Joe Dettling

Middle Row: Elizabeth, Frances, Leroy

Bottom Row: Geraldine Wendel Dettling, Helen, John Dettling Senior, holding John Dettling, Junior.

1992

Top Row left to right:
John Dettling Jr., Joe Dettling, Leroy Dettling

Bottom Row:
Helen Dettling Monfrey, Elizabeth Dettling Moreno, Frances Dettling Pullin

Elizabeth Moreno in the middle holding Chris and Ada in her lap, Michael and Patrick standing at her side

Moreno kids in pajamas: Patrick, Michael holding Chris, Ada Marie 1976

2020: Moreno's: Gabriel, Chris, Patrick, Ada, Michael

John and Geraldine Dettling 1992

John and Geraldine Dettling 2003

Introduction

Welcome to the roller coaster that was my world from 1971 till about 1979. These prayer poems chronicle the events in my life that led to happiness, heartbreak, joy, insecurity, optimism, poverty, hope, and above all, abiding trust in the goodness of our Heavenly Father.

In order to understand my journey, you need to know a little of the background.

I was raised in a Godly home, and although we were not wealthy by the world's standards, we did not lack. There was always food on the table, heat in our house, money coming in, hospitality for visitors, and encouragement along the way. With 6 siblings, we knew our responsibilities and we knew how to share. Needless to say, I had been fairly well protected from the craziness in the world of the 1960's.

I rarely dated in high school, so after I graduated in 1969, I took a job in the local donut shop and met the man who would impact my life forever. Although he had tattoos and was a drinker, I saw in him a need for someone to help him get his life in order. Mistakenly, I thought that person would be me. It was only much later that I discovered Jesus saves, and I didn't need to. By that time, I was in a miserable marriage with stair-step children... ages 1, 3,4, and 5. When people laughed and asked where "2" was, I replied, "It is now in heaven, with Jesus. It was a miscarriage."

Life was turbulent to say the least. We lived 10 miles from the nearest town of size and we did not always have a phone and running water. For at least three years, I had to carry water in gallon jugs to our house from a nearby water well or from my parent's house in Wharton. My babies bathed in a big wash tub unless we went to visit someone in town, usually my parents. My husband was a good worker when he wanted to be, but that was too irregular to count on. I didn't work outside the home because he kept me barefoot and pregnant.

Although I had graduated from Wharton County Junior College after we got married, my husband did not allow me to finish my education and really did not want me to have much contact with my old friends or family. I learned to live on beans and beans and more beans.

During this time, I cried out to Jesus and asked Him to save me just in case my Catholic upbringing didn't. My situation didn't change, but I did. A few months later, I got baptized in the Holy Spirit with the evidence of speaking in tongues. That gave me the strength I needed to persevere.

I tried my best to make our marriage work, but it takes two. After I had our 4th child, his daughter from his first marriage reentered our lives and the life we had did a downward spiral and he did all he could to make up for the 12 years of neglecting her. He neglected us instead.

One day, he left to get some propane for our cook stove and never came back. After he left, I stayed home with our four little ones, without a phone or working car, 10 miles from town. After about 3 days, my parents showed up and gave me the ultimatum… "Either come with us and we will help you with the kids, or stay with him and you're on your own."

I was at the point where my pride was already shattered, so I gave in to their demands. I packed what little we had and moved to town with my folks. The help they promised was there, but it was not the way I expected.

First of all, dad found a ramshackle house near Wharton to rent for us for $65 a month. It was a half a mile off the highway with a dirt road. If it rained, we were either in or out... there was no in-between. Some parts of the house had holes in the floor that were so big daylight would shine through. We ended up living there for about 5 months.

Later, the kids and I moved into government housing, after we had spent a couple of weeks in another house that had humongous holes in the roof. While we lived there, I heard cat calls when I came home late at night after working at the telephone company. We got out of there as quickly as we could.

After a couple of days, Dad took me to all the welfare agencies he could think of in our town. His message to the workers was, "My daughter's husband left her with these 4 children. I'm an old man already. What are you going to do to help them?" I felt smaller than 2 inches with all of his begging. I knew God would take care of us and I didn't need to beg, but there was no way to convince Dad of that.

I did eventually get help with food stamps and government housing, and I worked an assortment of jobs... in fact I worked 5 jobs at the same time during one part of my life. My first job was as a telephone operator, a second as a Welcome Wagon Woman, a third as a janitor for my church, a fourth as telephone salesperson for Olan Mills Portrait Studios, and I think I worked part time in sales at the local cable tv station.

Needless to say, I met myself coming and going.

While I was busy juggling jobs, I had to juggle my kids, too. Babysitters were expensive unless I left them with a relative... usually my parents or sister. Some of my children were already in either kindergarten or preschool and the baby had an at-home babysitter until my mom was able to take him. I had to learn to coordinate all these activities so our lives would run smoothly, or at least be not quite so bumpy.

I don't remember exactly when I started writing during that marriage, but when I did, it was therapeutic. These psalms take you through the highs and the lows and the in-betweens during that turbulent time. I'm sharing now in the hopes that God will be glorified.

Trust in the Lord with all your heart

And do not lean on your own understanding.

In all your ways acknowledge Him,

And He will make your paths straight.

Proverbs 3:5, 6

New American Standard Bible

Table of Contents

1.	1974	Mothers Lament
3.	January 6, 1974	The Religious Fanatic
5.	June 30, 1974	Mother's Love
7.	July 1, 1974	Finances are Low
8.	July 10, 1974	The Holy Spirit has Entered my
9.	July 10, 1974	Life The Dimpled Darling
10.	Unknown date	Building a Relationship with Jesus
14.	July 16, 1974	Overwhelmed
17.	July 23, 1974	Fears for the Future
19.	July 23, 1974	The Wannabe Poet
21.	July 28, 1974	The Happiness of Womanhood
24.	July 28, 1974	Poetic Inspirations
25.	July 28, 1974	Death of a Friendship
26.	July 29, 1974	Wash Day
27.	September 2, 1974	Disposable Babies
29.	September 28, 1974	For a Sick Child
30.	October 8, 1974	Six Month's
31.	October 9, 1974	The Joys of Being Broke
33.	October 11, 1974	Repo is Coming!
34.	October 14, 1974	Action Delayed
35.	October 14, 1974	Thanks for Driving in a Down Pour
36.	October 19, 1974	Reprieve Given

37.	October 28, 1974	His Cries for Independence
38.	October 25, 1974	Failure to take a Stand
39.	November 2, 1974	Why the Crop Failure?
41.	November 12, 1974	Keeping the Day Beautiful
43.	November 21, 1974	The Sunshine of Your Love
44.	December 9, 1974	The Joy of Your Love
45.	December 10, 1974	Raining in my Soul
46.	December 11, 1974	Why my Soul Cried
48.	Unknown date 1974	Crazy for Jesus
50.	January 1, 1975	Clueless
51.	January 31, 1975	Blessed by You
52.	February 19, 1975	The Faithfulness of Your Word
54.	April 1, 1975	Finally, a Home of our Own!
55.	May 1, 1975	A Car from my Daddy
56.	May 13, 1975	The Price of Being Self-Righteous
57.	May 23, 1975	Squirrel Cage Living.
58.	May 25, 1975	Rejoice!
59.	June 5, 1975	Litany of Life
63.	June 5, 1975	Peace in the Midst of the Storm
64.	July 31, 1975	True Christianity
67.	August 26, 1975	Morning
68.	September 20, 1975	The Greatness of God
70.	October 2, 1975	Thank You!
71.	October 2 1975	The Little things

73.	January 3, 1976	Our Provider
75.	January 6, 1976	Those Blessed Aches and Pains
77.	March 28, 1976	Thank You for Life
78.	Unknown date 1976	No Greater Love Unknown month
81.	August 22 1977	Life From A Child's Point Of View
82.	August 22, 1977	Precocious Pretenders
84.	August 24, 1977	Dear Father
86.	August 26, 1977	Giving my Petitions
88.	September 17, 1977	Fleeting Moments of Loneliness
90.	September 20, 1977	Cleansed by my Tears
91.	September 27, 1977	Evening Gone Awry!
92.	October 4, 1977	The Sacrifice of a Smile
94.	October 15, 1977	Metamorphosis
96.	November 5, 1977	Praying for my Husband
98.	December 1, 1977	Suppressing Loneliness
99.	December 27, 1977	Breakthrough?
100.	Unknown date, 1977	A New Game
103.	February 25, 1978	Satellite
104.	November 2, 1978	9:30pm Uptight!
107.	November, 1978	Memories
109.	August 1, 1979	Your Wandering Child
111.	1979 (approx.)	Broken Heart Mender
113.	**Part 2 Other Reflections On Life In Prose Song, And Poetry**	
114.	The Miracle from the Tithe	

116.	Jesus Protected Us in Apartment 77
119.	Kicked off Welfare to Buy a House
123.	Using the Foolish to Confound the Wise
127.	Keep on Trucking!
131.	I Remember Going Back to College
133.	Detoured to Israel by Way of Junior High.
137.	How I Met Helen Colin
140.	My Husband, Gabino (Gabby) Moreno Jr.
143.	Momma's Kitchen
149.	In Honor of John Dettling, Sr.
153.	In Honor of Helen Dettling Monfrey
155.	In Honor of Edmunda Wendel
158.	Lazarus Came Forth.
160.	Even the Dogs
164.	I'm Royalty!.
165.	My King My Lord
167.	Catch The Wind
169.	He Won't Ride a Donkey that Last Ride.
171.	Awesome!
172.	Jesus, You're Amazing!
174.	The Grass Withers
175.	A Mother's Christmas Story
178.	Momma's Easter Story

180.	Out on the Pier August 8, 2005
182.	Saved from the Clutches of Pharaoh
184.	Anniversary Tale
189.	She Dances in Her Dreams
191.	The Old Soldier
193.	Give Your Flowers
194.	Night Vision
195.	Are You Ready?
197.	The Smoke Writer in the Sky
199.	How Aglow Started in Wharton, Texas
202.	My Involvement in the Holocaust Remembrance Association
204.	Afterword

1974
Mothers Lament

Motherhood.

Sometimes, Lord, I wonder why

You ever created such a ...a... what?

Position? State of mind? Responsibility?

How could feeble humanity ever be equipped

to handle constant cries of

"I'm thirsty!" at 11 at night

or "The puppy just threw the toilet paper

in the toilet." Lord, You've entrusted

these little ones to me.

and sometimes, I'm so overwhelmed

by their choruses of "I'm thirsty!"

and "I'm hungry,"

and "I want a new toy!"

that I'd like to scream out,
"Kings X, Leave Me Alone!"
But I know that would never do.
I guess You get tired too, Lord.
We get awfully caught up in crying out to You
when we have problems.
Seems like we spend so much time whining,
we couldn't hear You answer
even if You spoke aloud.
Do we cry out because we want You?
Or because we enjoy the noise we make?
Lord, let me learn from the little ones.
Help me realize YOU are in control,
and You WILL answer!
Help me
to be still
and know that You are God!

January 6, 1974
The Religious Fanatic

Dear Lord Jesus,
I've done some reflecting today,
and I've come to a humbling decision ...
I see now that I know where to turn
when we've got troubles,
but I forget Who to thank - - -
and I mean REALLY thank - - -
when they're cleared up.
Lord, I've neglected You.
I've been a self - pitying, self - righteous,
fanatically religious donkey,
(and You know I mean worse than a donkey)
I keep asking, asking, asking,
and thanking, thanking, thanking,
but the thanking has been more out of
manners than true sincerity. I have been
thankful, Lord, but not the kind of thankful
that really pleases You.
I write constantly words that sound holy.

and I feel holy reading them.
But really living what I write
of is another thing.
Help me to be true to You
in all that I say and do.

Amen!

June 30, 1974
Mother's Love

I wonder... Do other mothers feel as I do
when they watch their children play?
Does joy swell within them
as their babes sleep?
Do they know how precious
their little lives are?
I do, Lord, and I am saddened to think
that some mothers know
their children starve
while they can only watch.
Their joy is dead.
There is no longer a need
to comfort them from their pains.
No need to calm them after shots.
No need to fulfill any simple pleasure
Lord, I'm lucky!
We are broke, but we are whole.
We feel pain, but we know joy.
We lack things, but we have You.

Lord, forgive us
For forgetting to be thankful.
Forgive us, Lord,
For not trusting Your goodness.
Help us, Lord,
To be more caring;
Thank You, Lord, for being near,
Thank You, Lord, for being You.

July 1, 1974
Finances are Low

Finances, Lord, are low.
I'm surprised how quickly they go.
We have little to eat,
No bread and no meat,
But we live in the hope of Your love

Our creditors come left and right.
I have nightmares about them at night
My excuses run thin,
Then I give them again,
but we live through faith

Help us, o Lord, to see
How to be financially free.
Give us a way to clear bills away
Then we'll proclaim the fruit of Your love.

July 10, 1974
The Holy Spirit has Entered my Life

The Holy Spirit has entered my life
to increase my joy and lessen my strife

He has cleansed my world from beginning to end
I don't want to be without Him again.

My burdens are gone, my worries are few.
My outlook on life is refreshing and new.

His love for me fills my heart so greatly
God only knows I want to be saintly.

Dearest Holy Spirit, help me, I plead Thee,
Lead me safely to God eternally.

July 10, 1974
The Dimpled Darling

What little boy
Grins like a possum,
Drinks from bottles
And like to toss 'em?
Shows his dimples
Cheek to cheek,
Makes life move faster
Week to week?
Little brother
Is that little brat.
He makes us run
And gives us laughs.
Never a dull moment
with him around.
He certainly is a little clown.

Building a Relationship with Jesus

One morning in March, 1974, as I listened to the *700 Club*, I realized my real need for Jesus as my Savior. I knelt to pray with Pat Robertson and confessed my sins, and they were many. I began with this statement... "Lord, I would like to think I would go to Heaven if I were to die now, but I'm not so sure I would. So just in case, Lord, I want to confess that I am a sinner and I want Jesus to be my Lord and Savior. Please, Lord, forgive me for my sins and accept me as your child. Amen!" My situation didn't change but I did.

I had my baby girl just a few weeks later, so now I had three under the age of four. One lady saw me later at a church bazaar and told me, "You look so good! What are you doing to make you so different?" I told her motherhood must be agreeing with me, but I realized later it was the difference that Jesus was making in my life.

Because of my newfound life in Christ, I wanted all He had to offer. I especially wanted to be baptized in the Holy Spirit, so I went to as many church services and prayer meetings as I could, seeking this gift. I went through all kinds of prayer lines where people laid hands on me, touched my throat and or stomach or whatever variety of methods they thought of, trying to help me receive this gift. Nothing visible happened and although I was left frustrated in my quest, I kept seeking.

By the time July rolled around, my hunger had increased and my quest continued. My Aunt Edmunda, who was a mentally challenged adult, listened to the *700 Club* with me and after they talked about Jesus and new life in Him, she asked me if I believed all that stuff. I happily replied, "Yes, I sure do!" And then my opportunity arrived...

Pat began teaching about how to receive the Baptism in the Holy Spirit. I was washing dishes with one hand, holding my 18-month-old son on my hip with the other, and listening for my baby girl in the bedroom, but my ears perked up and I paid full attention to what he said.

"It's like this," he said, "you ask me for $10 and tell me how desperately you need it. I reach in my pocket and get out a $10 bill and stretch out my hand to give it to you. You look at me with distress in your eyes and tell me, 'Pat, you don't understand! I have to have $10 and I need it right now!' Again, I tell you, 'Here it is... take it!' By now, you are frantic... 'Pat, please! I have to have $10!!!' I continue to hold out the money and you continue to act as though it's not there. You will never get that $10 until you reach out and take it. It's the same way with the Baptism of the Holy Spirit, YOU have to reach out and take it!"

Well, I had had some strange sounds rolling around in my head, but I thought the devil was trying to pull one over on my, so I ignored them. However, that particular morning, I decided to speak them out. Wow! I could not imagine what was getting ready to happen... I spoke in a foreign language!!!

"Abba delia sancti, ..." I started out and continued flowing in unknown phrases to praise my God. I could literally feel the outburst flowing like bubbles from my innermost being. Words gushed and I tried really hard not to frighten my aunt with my new tongue. I decided to use checking my toddler's diaper in the bedroom as an excuse to see if my language was still working. Glory to God, it was!

The first time I did that and came back into the kitchen, I looked out the window and saw three eggs in the yard. "Hallelujah!" I thought, "What a blessing!" so I went out and picked them up and went to check my baby's diaper again...and the prayer language still flowed. So, I came to the kitchen a second time and again looked out the window.

There were three more eggs! "Lord, you are so good! Thank you for the eggs. You know how much we need them for food!" After I gathered them the second time, I had to check the baby's diaper again in the other room and I could still pray in an unknown tongue.

What a surprise I received again after coming back into the kitchen! Three more eggs were out in the yard! I was overwhelmed with thankfulness because the Lord was showering me with His blessings on that eventful day. The very fact that I found three eggs on three separate occasions on the day that I received the blessing of the Third Person of the Holy Trinity was a true miracle for many reasons, but Jesus used these events to confirm His love for me. It was all the greater because we didn't even have chickens and as far as I knew, our neighbors didn't either.

I found out later that someone's dog had brought them up, but the very fact that he brought three at a time without breaking them must have been a God thing. Whatever way they got there, I thanked God wholeheartedly because I really didn't know what I would be serving for supper that night because we were really poor. I ended up scrambling those blessed eggs for supper and praised The Lord with every bite.

That encounter with Jesus and the Holy Spirit changed my life and equipped me to face greater difficulties that would arise. Although it's been so many years ago, that experience is as fresh on my mind as if it were yesterday. Jesus has held on to me ever since and I praise Him for His faithfulness.

July 16, 1974
Overwhelmed

The house is a mess, Lord.
I need to clean and mop and dust and sweep.
I've got sewing to do and
toys to straighten,
But I just wanted to let You know that I know You care.
You see, Lord,
Sometimes I get all wrapped up
in these earthly chores.
They seem to overwhelm me,
And I lose perspective and
forget what really matters.
Oh, I know, Father, they matter as
far as the world goes,
and it is awful hard to live comfortably
in a human pig pen.
But Lord, I get so tired
of the same old dishes
and the same old broom,
and the diapers,

and the building blocks and the ironing.
Day after day after day after day...
Sometimes I want a release,
to turn back time
or move it forward.
or be anywhere
but here and now.
And then my little ones smile
or say, "I'm Mommy's baby!"
or my husband compliments me,
and somehow,
the troubles are gone.
Not really, though,
but they are diminished.
And Lord, that helps,
Because if they don't seem as big,
They're easier to get through.
It is said that
"Cleanliness is next to Godliness."
But the Bible says God is love.
And Love is something
have plenty of!

Thank you, Father, for Your love.
I know it will see me through.
Amen!

July 23, 1974
Fears for the Future

I wonder, Lord, what the future holds.
I know what was yesterday, and is
today, but what of our tomorrows?
Will my children
stay fed and healthy?
Or will they, too,
be part of the really famished?
I worry. Yes, Lord, I worry a lot!
I know, deep inside,
You WILL see us through.
Today we have groceries
and soaps and towels
that by other people's standards
are things that they take for granted.
But when I hear
of the woes of foreign nations,
I almost feel guilty for what we do
have, And wonder when we
will join their ranks.

I'm grateful, Lord, so very grateful,
that You have protected us from
hunger and kept us well.
You have kept our children healthy,
And full of the Love of Life that is You.
Thank You, Lord.
You are our Shepherd.
Our trust is in You.
Amen!

July 23, 1974
The Wannabe Poet

Look at me.
I sit here, acting the poet;
Me, the mother of three.
Me, wife of a junk man-
Me, daughter of a barber-
Me, unlikely woman, with words unspoken.
I sit here, trying to be eloquent,
and in my vanity, it sounds so.
My mind is afire with blazes of phrases.
I conjure images equal to any poet's!
And yet, what is a poet?
Have I no humility?
Do I deserve a position of such prestige?
Ha! I write for myself,
My own selfish needs.
I let my soul run free;
my pen goes wild.
Maybe I'll share these things...
maybe someday I'll be famous!

But for now,

I'll be content to be selfish.

What I write is for me and the Man upstairs.

He understands, and even if it isn't poetic,

or rhythmic, or onomatopoetic.

He accepts it.... perhaps others will too.

He deserves more than these feeble efforts,

yet I know He understands.

July 28, 1974
The Happiness of Womanhood

Today he gave me a compliment.
Well, not exactly,
but to me, it was from Heaven.
An anti-libber was on TV,
A HOW woman,
Extolling the joys of womanhood:
the honors of American females;
the blessings of a USA wife;
the privileges of here and now.
And he laughed at her.
Wonder of wonders,
HE LAUGHED!
"If only she knew you!" is what he
said... What he meant was,
"If only she did what you do,
she'd change her mind!"
My Lord! he's noticed!!!
The trips to the water well,
the unconnected faucets...

the mown grass...
the slopped hog...
the hand washed diapers...
the home canned foods...
the scrubbed floors...
the boiled water...
the useless commode...
the enamel potty...
the non-running car...
the empty bank account...
the usually bare freezer...
the homemade bread...
the do-it-yourself mixes.
Yes, Lord, he's really noticed!
I've always thought
that he thought women have it too easy.
And I KNEW he included me.
Boy, was I wrong!!!
And I'm glad!
His laugh was music to my ears.
But what he doesn't know
is that despite this list
(and more)

I've loved it all.
It's been for him
and our babies
and our future.
And isn't that
The real joy of
womanhood?

July 28, 1974
Poetic Inspirations

Poetic inspirations...
It's amazing how they come,
Little things throughout the day
Seem to make them run.

All the things that happen,
The things I do and see,
Give ideas like little lights
That mean a lot to me.

My children, my husband,
My faith, and my strife
Cause me to write
Of the things in my life.

I hope that one day
When these things I share
Folks lives will be blessed
And they'll know that I care.

July 28, 1974
Death of a Friendship

The death of a friendship can be a sad thing.

You'll know it's happened by talk's hollow ring.

Old comrades will smile and greet you with glee.

But talks of the past are all so empty

Bonds once so strong are weakened by time.

The old strength of unions no longer can bind.

Must friendships end this way? Must they die with time?

If not cared for carefully, They're dead past their prime.

(My best friend from high school could not understand the changes that had taken place in my life and pulled back from our relationship. She told me about a book called *I'm Okay, You're Okay* and that supposedly explained our rift. However, many years later, she encountered Jesus and the Holy Spirit as I had. Our friendship went deeper than ever as we reunited and she grew in the spirit so rapidly that I almost felt the dust as she sped on with the faith she had come to accept. She went to be with Jesus as a result of breast cancer in 2010. I miss her still, but praise God for the time He gave me with her, especially as sisters in the Lord.)

July 29, 1974
Wash Day Pride

Flags of freedom in the wind,
woman's washday pride.
Dancing gaily in the breeze,
like the ebbing of the tide.

Bath towels clean blow freshly
new, nighties spotless glow;
Faded blue jeans bright again, old
diapers white like snow.

Is this every woman's dream?
No, I dare to say.
But these flags of freedom
are the joy of my washday.

September 2, 1974
Disposable Babies

My dear Lord!
Is this what we've come to?
From controlled cycles and
Throw away sperm,
we now dispose of living flesh and blood.
How, Lord? And why?
Is life not more precious
than just something for an incinerator?
My skin crawls and my stomach churns
to imagine such sights.
And yet I know they are real.
If I could, Lord,
I would take all of these little ones into my breast.
I would caress them as I now caress my own,
and say, "You are loved! You are wanted!
You are a child of God!"
But how can I, Lord? How?
Take them all to Yourself, Father,

Let these uncompleted but perfected
lives lead their mothers to You.
Please, Lord, re-arrange their values.
Show them the way.
Show them that all life,
even these unborn innocents,
is Your life.
Please, Father, I pray in Jesus name.
Amen!

September 28, 1974
For a Sick Child

It's getting to me, Lord.
I mean my baby's sick,
And I can't do a damn thing about it.
It hurts me so bad
to see her suffer.
She's so little, Lord,
and so hungry.
Diarrhea seems minor, but after a week,
it's downright serious.
She cries from the pain
and I can only cry back in my pain for her.
Help her, Lord.
Please, Father, help her!
My tears won't make her well.
Your healing touch can.
You WILL take care of her!
You MUST! ... no one else can!!!
Even in my doubts of You, I have faith in You.
Forgive my disbelief. Give fruit to my trust.
Remember us, Lord! Thank You! Amen!

October 8, 1974
Six Month's Praises

"6 months" has such happy sounds -
the coos and droolings and shrieks
are so melodic to a loving ear.
They sound like the "tongues" of infancy
that praise You endlessly.
So happy, so trusting, so full of life.
Help me to be like her, Lord.
Help me to be happy being me.
Let the sounds of my day
be as pleasing to You as the sounds of
hers. Let me praise You with my all,
as unashamedly as she does.
Thank you, Father!

Amen

October 9, 1974
The Joys of Being Broke

It's not so bad to be broke, Lord.

In fact, it's really quite an experience!

I've gotten new insights to life

and have discovered things I never knew existed...

like payment reminders and bill collectors...

water well trips and phoneless living.

Why, if it weren't for being broke,

I'd have never become friends with some neighbors who

have phones and running water.

I'd never have known how far I

can stretch a pound of hamburger

or a bar of soap.

Never learned how to cook a good pot of beans

or make waffles from scratch.

And most of all, I'd have never been able to empathize

with those who honestly ARE poor!

and that's important,

Because, Lord, I know our brokenness is from paycheck to paycheck

and someday, the paycheck will be all ours.

But the others, Lord,
don't have the hope I have.
They need Your security.
I can dream of the little things I want
and I feel like a queen as I get them.
But the others do well to eat from day to
day, much less dare to dream.
But they need a reminder from You.
Let them know that they, too,
are Your lilies of the valley.
Thanks, Lord. Amen!

October 11, 1974
Repo is Coming!

Lord, we need a miracle mighty fast!
Today's Friday and if we don't get one by Monday,
our trailer is gonna get up and go.
Our last payment got lost somewhere
along the way to the company
so the repo man is supposed to haul our home away
Boy! What a way to go!!!
Right now, I feel a little like laughing,
because I am all cried out.
But I kind of feel like You have something planned for us or
else this wouldn't have happened.
And no matter how much I would like to keep this old tin can
a while yet,
I'll let it go cheerfully,
as long as I know it's Your will.
After all, You are STILL in control.
Thanks, whatever You decide.

October 14, 1974
Action Delayed

Well, Lord, today is Tuesday
And we still have our home.
Can it be that You HAVE
worked out a miracle?
And I thank You for it,
and praise You for it.
The fact that we are still in here
Is a miracle.
They changed haul-away date
to Wednesday or Thursday,
And it is no telling
what You have in store for us by then.
I feel relief, Lord, that You are caring
for us. Thank you for everything.

October 14, 1974
Thanks for Driving in a Down Pour

You drove for me yesterday, Lord.
I didn't take time to tell You
how much I appreciated Your help.
I couldn't have made it through that blinding
rain (without windshield wipers) otherwise.
When I got out of the downpour,
I could hardly believe
the darkness I saw behind me.
I asked for Your help
and You gave it abundantly,
even to keeping the babies still
while "we" drove!
Thank You for Your help.
I appreciate it and love You for it. Amen!

October 19, 1974
Reprieve Given

You've done it again, my Lord!

A whole week has gone by since our eviction notice

and this trailer is still our home.

Do You know, Lord,

I was prepared to be out of here,

if You had intended?

I was packed and boxed

and mentally attuned to be moved,

but in Your wisdom and goodness,

You've kept us here, and we are grateful, Lord.

You understood our dilemma

and worked out the answer!

You are the GREATEST, Lord!

Thank You, Jesus, and PTL!

(The trailer did eventually get repossessed, but by that time, we were already in a house that my husband had built for us. The house wasn't grand and glorious, but it provided shelter and it was sturdy enough to stand up to the winds and the rain.)

October 28, 1974
His Cries for Independence

Jesus,
Why does "3" aggravate me so?
Why do I resent his cries of independence?
And defiance of me?
He's only doing what comes naturally
and I find myself seething with anger.
My patience at times is stretched
like a rubber band ready to pop,
and I don't know how to cope.
I can't give in to his every whim
and I can't punish him for every "wrong" he does.
He must do these things if he is to grow-
this experience is needed.
But my nerves aren't always prepared.
Help me, oh Lord, to understand him.
Build my patience and help me to accept
and guide his declarations of independence.
Give me the love I need
to see him through these times that try both of us.
Thank You!
AMEN!

October 25, 1974
Failure to take a Stand

Lord, forgive me for the times
I lack courage to witness for You...
Like when unholy things come on tv or radio
And I do not turn it off or change channels
or ignore them completely
Or when someone is gossiping
And do not remind them of You.
I am ashamed of my weakness and lack of
boldness. I need and I want Your courage, Jesus.
Give me Your protection and
keep me under Your wing.
Do not let these things spoil me for Your Kingdom
Nor invade my spirit
like demons looking for a home.
Perfect my imperfection. Guide me with Your
light, and lead me safely home to You. Amen

November 2, 1974
Why the Crop Failure?

Dear Lord,
Why am I having crop failure
instead of a bumper crop?
I've planted seed in so many places
but I've seen no fruit yet.
I've written letters galore
sharing the good news
of my infilling and salvation,
but that's gotten no results.
I've given money out of our need,
expecting 10-fold,
but we've gotten no more than usual.
I've attempted selling some writing
to fulfill the saying,
"The Lord helps those who help themselves"
and still, nothing!
Lord, I'm getting overanxious...

I'm getting uptight, waiting for my due season.
I want to see the fruit of my seed
pressed down, shaken together, and flowing
over. I want to --- need to -— see it soon!
Please, Lord, hear me!
Build my faith.
Let me see the results soon.
In dear Jesus' Name. Amen!

November 12, 1974
Keeping the Day Beautiful

Lord,
It's such a beautiful day!
I could ruin it so easily
by dwelling on our financial
negatives. But I won't...
I'll make it as perfect as I can
by thinking of the positives:
like good health and warmth
and food and shelter;
like the friendship of Your children
and the fullness of life;
like the million-dollar smiles and free
spirits in my babies;
like the greenness of the grass
and the freshness of the breeze;
like the briskness of the air
and the friskiness of Your critters.

So many, many things that money can't
buy. Keep me mindful of these gifts of
Yours, Lord Jesus.
They are more wonderful
than words can express.
They are a panacea
that only You can give.
Thank You, Lord!
Amen!

November 21, 1974
The Sunshine of Your Love

Dear Lord,

The sunshine today is

so like the warmth of Your love-

comforting strong, reassuring.

It feels as though it's a blanket enveloping

me, protecting me from the chill, and evils

of life, And it's a feeling of love.

Its brightness is like Your brightness,

Almost blinding at times,

But always needed in order to see.

Keep me under the blanket of Your love,

Let me stay warm in Your protection.

Thank You, precious Father.

December 9, 1974
The Joy of Your Love

Jesus, I feel so full of You today!
You are bubbling inside me
and I find myself singing
and dancing in Your joy!
And I want to share Your gifts to me
with everyone.
Lord, You're wonderful!
I don't deserve such happiness,
but I'm grateful for it.
You've worked so many miracles
for me already that I've lost track.
Thank You, precious Brother,
Dear Father, Sweet Spirit,
I will stay mindful of Your loving
goodness and I will do what I can to
spread it around. Amen! Alleluia!!!

December 10, 1974
Raining in my Soul

Oh, Lord, my Lord,
it's raining today and it's raining in my soul.
Christmas is coming
and I, like the little drummer boy,
have nothing to give but myself.
I know that's a terrible thing to say,
and I don't like myself for saying it,
but how do you tell a child
Santa Claus isn't coming?
And how do you explain to close kin
that you're not being cheap
when you give something simple?
Lord, help me!!!
Don't let me give in to that defeated
feeling. Show me a way to make the most
of the little I have.
Let me put in as much of myself - and You-
as I can, down to the last measure.
Please, Lord, I plead! Amen

December 11, 1974
Why my Soul Cried

I know why my soul cried yesterday, Lord.
It wasn't just Christmas giving —
It was something going from my life...
the little one I'll never hold.
The little one I didn't know existed.
Lord, I know you answer prayer,
and I know you work in strange ways.
But why did my baby have to go?
I loved it, Lord!
Even in its nothingness, loved it!
It was from You and it went back to You,
before I even had a chance to build bonds.
How can such a young thing
find perfection so quickly?
I know You are caring for it.
You love it more than I ever could.
Keep my baby safe for me, Jesus,
And introduce us when we get to heaven, okay?
Its brothers and sisters and daddy and mommy
Will join it when You are ready for us.

Keep us safe until that day.

Thank You, Lord.

Amen!

Unknown date 1974
Crazy for Jesus

Well, Lord, I think I've just been given
A backhanded compliment.
An older lady, a relative, sneered at me
as she derided my love for You.
"You must be crazy!" she said.
"You're acting like a nut!" she said.
"You're always talking about Jesus, Jesus, Jesus!"
"Don't you know how to talk about anything else?"
she said. And even though she thought
she was putting me down,
Her words let me know
That I must be doing something right.
I'm not sure, but I'm guessing my love for You
Caused her to feel guilty
for not having You in her life.
I didn't mean to cause her distress,
But having You in my life gives me peace.
I can only wish
that she could have that peace as well.

Yes, I may be crazy,
but it is a magnificent craziness,
because, Jesus, I'm crazy for You,
and I'm so glad I am!!!

January 1, 1975
Clueless

Lord, I am wrong to want him alone?
Just me and him, like the times so long ago?
No babies, no in-laws, no outlaws, no company, nobody?
Is it asking too much for a little real privacy
and togetherness after four years?
He doesn't understand this thing with me,
and maybe I have blown it out of proportion.
But, Lord, it hurts me until I become obnoxious
to him and myself and You.
I don't like to be hateful, but I am,
And I can't tell him what the real trouble is.
Messiness is one way of fighting back,
but it only causes me more trouble.
Oh, Lord, help me to change!
Help me to appreciate the few times we do have.
Clue him in on my wants and maybe things will be better.
Please, Lord? We need Your touch. Amen!

January 31, 1975
Blessed by You

My Lord, I feel so loved by You and blessed...
To be alive...To be a wife...To be a mother...
To be Your sister...And to be your daughter.
And especially blessed to have You!
I get exasperated at times
and wonder how near You really are,
and I have been tempted not to look,
but I haven't given in.
and Your love for me just grows and grows.
Thank You for 'babysitting' me
day in, day out, 24 hours a day.

February 19, 1975
The Faithfulness of Your Word

Lord, it's me again.

Full of awe at Your wonderful plan for life,

especially my life with You.

I don't know how You've done it, Lord,

and I really don't care.

But You've worked more miracles

and I'm astounded!

It seems that by now

I should be grown enough in faith

to accept Your work,

but still You amaze me constantly.

You've given us a chance to clear our financial woes.

I won't say I hope it pans out this time...

I will say it will work this time

Because You ordained it.

Thank You, Lord.

You've answered another prayer, too, my Jesus.

You've sent me a real live prayer partner

And I've learned again to trust

In the faithfulness of your Word.
Lord, I knew You would do it.
I didn't know who, or how, or when,
When she came, she had pains in her leg,
And as we prayed, newly conscious
of our sisterhood in Christ,
You healed her.
Thank You, precious Jesus.
You've given me renewed faith in my Father.
Thank You with all my heart.
Amen.

April 1, 1975
Finally, a Home of our Own!

Jesus, I'm happy.
We're in our home now,
our very own home,
and You've done it for us.
You've given us not only two stoves
and an ice box,
but a table and six chairs.
And three beds and shelves and hanging
space and storage space and curtains and
two rugs. Some worldly people might think
I'm crazy to be satisfied with this.
But I am content, because I know
You're with us every step of the way,
it's not fancy, by any means,
and the warmth is more from Your love
than the stove.
But it's ours and it's home and it's from You,
Thank You, Jesus.

May 1, 1975
A Car from my Daddy

Dear Jesus,

I got my car today from Daddy, although my
Father really gave it to me.
Lord, before I get mileage on it,
I'm going to dedicate it to You,
To Your greater honor and glory.
Anything I can do for You, Lord,
Because of this car, I will do.
Let me use it to spread Your word.
Let this car cause no evil.
And let it only be a chariot of good will.
Dear Lord, it's Yours!
Dear Father, thank You
For guiding my Daddy in getting it
And thank You for letting my husband agree.
To God be the glory for this major miracle.
Amen! Alleluia!!!

May 13, 1975
The Price of Being Self-Righteous

Lord Jesus,

I feel rotten,

as though I'm sapping Your life from me

by the words that have been coming from my lips.

Lord, how can I be so self-righteous

that I can condemn others

but better myself at the same time?

Forgive me, Jesus, I've been such a louse,

gloating in the shortcomings of others.

When will I learn?

Lord, that if You forgave and didn't cast stones,
that I shouldn't either?

Where is Your love in me when I do such a thing?

Oh, Lord, with the words of my mouth

I have been destroying Your life in me and I feel the pain.

Jesus, I do forgive the others

for they don't know what they're doing.

Lead my heart in following You

and my lips in speaking Your words.

Thank You, Jesus. Amen!

May 23, 1975
Squirrel Cage Living

Lord, I've been in a doldrum.

I've got things to do,

and it seems so useless at times.

I'm on a treadmill that won't stop,

Like a caged squirrel running, with no place to go.

Why is it, Lord, that I feel so defeated so often?

Why can't I have more victory?

Or is it I have the victory,

And just haven't proclaimed it?

I let little things bug me

until I'm infested with negativism.

Then it plagues me for days on end.

Lord, help me!

Saturate me with the salve of Your love.

I NEED Your energizer!!!

Fill me, Lord! Amen!

May 25, 1975
Rejoice!

Rejoice with me, my brothers and sisters,

The Lord, our God,

has His hand upon my husband and children.

He protects them with His might

from the snare of the evil one.

He keeps them from harm,

and saves them for Himself.

He guides them daily

and sends bands of angels to ward off danger.

My God is a good God to all who call upon His

Name. Praise the Lord and bless His holy Name

forever Amen!

June 5, 1975
Litany of Life

Lord,
There are so many times in life that I need You
to get me through the day;
so many times I'm too perturbed or upset to ask Your help,
too involved or unbelieving to step back and let You take over;
O, Lord, in times like these,
remember this litany and come to my aid.
When I've punished the kids for little spats,
Lord, let me love them.
When Big Brother spills his fourth glass of milk for the day,
Lord, let me love him.
When Little Brother wets his pants on purpose,
Lord, let me love him.
When Princess tears my mail to bits,
Lord, let me love her.
When hubby wakes me from a sound sleep
to get him a snack while he watches tv,
Lord, let me love him.
When I need a babysitter
and I'm given a flippant "no",

Lord, let me love her.
When I'm cooking a meal and
Princess clings to my legs,
Lord, let me love her.
When I've told Big Brother to wait a few minutes
for whatever, and he keeps nagging anyway,
Lord, let me love him.
When Little Brother lets the pups have his
sandwich, Lord, let me love him.
When Princess wets her didee after she's sat on
the potty effortlessly for 15 minutes,
Lord, let me love her.
When Big Brother helps himself to what he wants
and causes trouble in the process,
Lord, let me love him.
When hubby has used all the gas from the car
and I'm left stranded,
Lord, let me love him.
When Little Brother brings in a bucket of sand
and dumps it on the just-made bed,
Lord, let me love him.
When I'm ignored completely by people I care for,
Lord, let me love them.

When the oldsters at the nursing home
tell me their stories for the jillionth time,
Lord, let me love them.
When people don't want to listen
to my stories about You,
Lord, let me love them.
When the dogs kill the chickens,
Lord, let me love them.
When I have ten thousand things to do at once,
Lord, give me peace.
When I have a sick child
and can't help his problems,
Lord, give me peace.
When we are out of water and
I need to make extra trips to the well,
Lord, give me peace.
When I have to choose between household
chores and daughterly duties,
Lord, give me peace.
When Big Brother bugs me while I read or
write, Lord, give me peace.
When I am tired and can't rest,
Lord, give me peace.

So many times throughout the day
I find myself needing Your help
And knowing I can't make it without You
When that happens, Lord,
Thank You for Your intervention,
Your peace, and Your ability to love,
No matter how overwhelmed I am.
I place my total trust and confidence in You.

June 5, 1975
Peace in the Midst of the Storm

Lord, it's raining outside. One baby's sleeping,
the others' going to sleep, and the third is quiet.
Such peace is rare!
So, Lord, I'm taking this chance to thank you.
Lord, our financial problems are clearing up
slowly but surely.
I've got a few new clothes,
we've got two running cars in good condition,
and we've got groceries.
That's more than we've had in an awful long time!!!
Lord Jesus,
Your goodness overwhelms me!
You do look out for Your own,
Dear Lord.
All we had to do was trust in Your Word.
Thank You, Jesus.
Maranatha! Amen!!!

July 31, 1975
True Christianity

Lord, someone asked me,
"What is being a good Christian?"
Is it doing things to earn brownie points
for Heaven, so you don't go to hell?
Is it doing loving acts
even when they feel hypocritical?
How do I know I'm going there?
My Dear Lord,
How do I answer these things?
I know we must be born again.
You said that Yourself.
But when you do loving acts
as a matter of Brownie points
rather than heart feelings,
are they any less a ticket to Heaven?
Or do they add coals to hells fire?
I've thought about that Lord,
and I've tried to answer.
Lord, it has to be that way.

We couldn't do things for others
without the thought
that You would do these things Yourself.
And the only way we can do these things
is through Your spirit
because man's spirit is self-centered.
If You had thought like we think sometimes,
we would never have been saved from ourselves
or from the damnation of hell.
I'm not sure I believe in the fire and brimstone of hell,
my Jesus. But if there be such a place,
I don't want to go there.
I may not believe in it,
but I will live righteously as if it does exist.
I will join You in Heaven,
with my Father because I have accepted You.
Your Word says
that I will be with You
just as You are with me.
I may still have moments of weakness,
but I know beyond the shadow of a doubt
that what I have in me
by being born again through Your Spirit

is much greater than what is in the world. Thank you, Lord, for showing me the way. Help me to show it to others.

Praise You, Jesus!

Maranatha!

Amen!

AUGUST 26, 1975
Morning Gold

Morning gold in the sky,
shining bright - like You.
Just a taste of things to come,
like future life with You.
Glowing bright and beautiful,
giving rays of life
For those who recognize the
Source as Master of their lives.

September 20, 1975
The Greatness of God

Lord, it does things to me
to realize the scope of Your majesty.
To know that life
in every little ant or bee or bird or kitten
comes from the Source that my life is from.
To know that the same Being
that created fossils
millions of years ago
and the water springs deep inside the earth
and the mountains that go so high in the
heavens took time to create me.
It's really mind boggling, Lord, to know
that this same breath that flows through me
flowed through every person
or plant or animal ever since time began...
that every leaf that trembles in the wind
and every blossom that buds forth
and every root that spreads its tentacles
all share the same tender, loving care

from the same Maker.
Lord, You're wonderful!
Thank You for letting me be
and thank You for letting me
know the greatness of You.
Amen!

October 2, 1975
Thank You!

Thanks, Lord,

for being big enough for me to share.

Thanks for filling my life,

taking it over, for inebriating me with You.

And everyone else who has accepted Your

love. Thank You, Jesus!

Amen!!

October 2 1975
The Little things

I'm so grateful, Lord, for the little things.
Even though I don't shout Your praise at the
time, I think of them constantly
and accept them all as miracles
from You to me with love.
Like the dormant tomato vines that have grown
fruitlessly all summer, and now,
in the face of October chill,
tomatoes lie clustered in many branches.
Like the pull rope on the lawnmower.
I couldn't do it... the 8 horsepower
was too much for me,
and a half hour later,
when I decided to try again,
I gave the pull to You,
and, as always, You came through.
Like the dead battery cables on the truck.
I couldn't get them operating,
but when I asked You to take over,
You did and it started immediately.

Lord, You are so wonderful to me!
I can only smile at Your goodness
and seek ways to share it.
and even now, other miracles flood my mind.
Like the nights my little one woke me
for me to take him to the potty.
Not many 18-month-old toddlers
would do that.
But maybe their mothers don't know You.
Like curing my baby of her diarrhea...
I worried and fretted in despair all week.
but when I finally broke down in written prayer,
You healed her without a doctor bill.
Like keeping burns from hurting me,
all the times I've touched
hot pots and pans.

I should be spotted from scars,
But I'm not... thanks to You.
So many times you've taken over.
You haven't failed me yet.
Thank You, Lord, for remembering me.
Thank You for the little things.
Amen!

January 3, 1976
Our Provider

Lord, I look around me and I see miracles.
Many more than I expected
and much more than I deserve.
Lord, You're so good to me.
I'm ready to cry thinking of Your loving
kindness. You've given us shelter ~
warm, comfortable, livable shelter.
Thank You, Jesus.
You've given us clothes
enough to outfit all of us
for weeks and weeks and then some.
Thank You, Jesus.
And You've given us food –
nutritious, filling assorted food.
Thank You, Jesus.
Father, You take such good care of us.
Your love overwhelms me.
Thank You for it all,
And, Lord, bless the people You've used

to provide these things for us, especially Grandma.

She has been an angel sent by You,

Thank You, Daddy God,

for her and all Your precious earthly family.

Amen. Maranatha!

January 6, 1976
Those Blessed Aches and Pains

My fourth little one is growing, Lord.
And making me very aware of his presence.
He must be a healthy one, for by days end,
my joints and ribs feel very crowded
and we have five months to go
before he is born.
Lord, I thank You for these aches and pains
that keep me so certain of his health
within my body.
I may complain and look for human sympathy,
but with every complaint, goes a silent
"Thank You, Jesus!"
Lord, I dedicate his entire life to You,
from his conception three months ago,
to his birth next summer,
to every tear and smile he gives in growing.
He's Yours, Lord.
I understand why You took our last one, Jesus.
We couldn't have provided for it as we should have.

but by Your grace and with Your help, We will care for this one quite well. Thank you, Father.

Help us as we need it.

Maranatha!

Amen!

March 28, 1976
Thank You for Life

Thank You, Lord, for springtime.
For new life within me,
in the gardens, and in creation.
Yes, even for 14 new puppies with hungry
tummies. Thank You for neighbor's cattle
that stray into our yard
because we can share their beauty.
Thank You for the hope of tomorrow.
Thank You for starry nights,
and rainy days, and rainy nights.
Thank you for children...
boisterous, happy, loving children.
Thank you for one-on-one relationships,
especially the love of a husband,
and the confidences of friends
Thank You for life, dear Jesus!
Most of all, thank You for You! Amen!

No Greater Love
Unknown month 1976

I fell in love once.
Once was all it took.
We joked and laughed, argued and cried.
Lord, we were in love!
He told me this... he told me that...
he told me something else...
And I believed him.
Like a little child, I believed him.
So we married.
School went... babies came... dreams faded.
Bills and burpings, dishes and diapers filled my
day. Old friends found greener pastures,
While I stayed in my own back yard.
I loved him still.
Babies doubled, bills did too.
And as times got harder, I worried...
About health... about money... about life.

Life was hard
and I was doing the best that I could
to make a go of it,
but I seemed to be getting stressed more and
more. Then one day, through my tears,
God gave me a revelation.
Even though I was offering my life
for someone who did not realize my sacrifice,
Someone greater had given His life for mine.
Someone died so that I might live.
Someone suffered the penalty for sin that was
mine, Someone died
so that I could reap the benefit of life eternal.
I saw that my suffering was temporary,
but the reward He sowed would be eternal.
It was then I realized that there was no greater
love than the love of my Savior
and I knew no matter how much I had given up,
I did not give up my home in Heaven
to come to Earth to save mankind.
Was my love the greatest love?
No, not even close.
My Savior Jesus is the One

Who showed no greater love,
and I am forever grateful!
He gave me grace to take one day at a
time, One challenge at a time,
And one sacrifice at a time.
And His love is still
the Greatest Love ever shown.

August 22 1977
Life From A Child's Point Of View

There's something about being three foot tall
that gives the whole world a different color.
You know, Lord, it's mighty easy
to see someone's tub of lard
hanging over his beltline
when it's on your eye level.
And the dried gum stuck under table tops
can be extremely fascinating.
A field of weeds turns into a deep, dark jungle
if you're shorter than the grass tops.
Lord, keep me mindful of the world through their
eyes. Help me to realize their needs and fears
and temptation and misconceptions.
Keep me in tune with them so I can be in tune with
You. Help me to talk to them, and not over them.
And most of all, dear Lord,
Help me to remember
that I trod their tracks not so long ago myself.
Amen.

August 22, 1977
Precocious Pretenders

Miniature people all around me.
Conversing, laughing, thinking, crying.
Are they so different from me, Lord?
They're so sure and unsure of themselves,
just like me.
They'll tackle anything
if they're given half a chance.
Is it really possible
to be such a nonexpert expert?
Treehouses are an easy task
for a five-year-old construction worker.
All he needs is a few boards, some nails,
a hammer, a few tree branches, and some imagination.
The VA might not approve a loan for him,
But the little man has his tree house
and didn't even need an architect.
Three-year-old mommies do quite well
without nine months of pregnancy, doctor visits,
and hospital stays.

Give her a few well-loved old dollies,
(there must be at least one
with a topnotch for carrying purposes).
And she has an instant family,
No hassle, no obligation, and no 2 am feedings.
A simple, dimpled, "I love you, Mommy!"
Can certainly soften the blows of correction
for the four-year-old
who has just colored the kitchen door.
Bribery becomes a subtle asset early in life.
Lord, I ask You to protect them.
I know You can't isolate them,
But You can insulate them
from the harshness of reality.
I just ask that somehow, some way,
that You keep them aware of your love and protection.
Let Your buoyancy keep them afloat
in the river of life.
Amen!

August 24, 1977
Dear Father

Dear Father,

I'm worn -—- mentally, physically,

and almost spiritually.

I don't like NOT knowing, but You know.

Maybe it's better

that I'm not omniscient as far as my husband goes.

But Lord, I can't help but wonder.

I have made him part of my life...

He is the daddy I chose for my children...

he is half of me.

Lord God,

You've given me so many promises

and reassurances for him.

I trust You, Lord, to be faithful to Your Word.

You told me he will be saved and filled with Your

Holy Spirit.

I believe You.

Help my unbelief, Lord.

If and when his world caves in on him,

be there to catch him.

I have relinquished him to You

by filing the divorce papers.

I know You're in control

and I know what the end will be,

but I need to know Your presence now.

Thank You for renewing my strength from

within. Thank You for the material blessings

You've given me,

And especially, thank You for You!

In Jesus' name I pray,

August 26, 1977
Giving my Petitions

Father God,
I'm so helpless, so nothing without You.
You have said to make our request know to You.
I know, Father, that You know what I need.
But I will list my requests specifically to You in
the name of Jesus,
That You may answer them.
Food for my children and me or
money to buy the food stamps.
Detergent for clothes ~ bleach and softener,
too! Propane for the heater and stove
Money to pay the phone bill
Money to pay the light bill
Money to pay the stove off
or a good used stove to replace this one
A lawnmower
A chopping hoe and shovel
Cat food and dog food
new shoestrings or shoes for the kids

reliable, roomy transportation
I'm overwhelmed, Lord!
I have no one to turn to except You.
Please Father, send Your answer quickly.
I won't go begging,
but I expect Your provision.
I claim it, and I thank You for it.
And I do ask in the name of Your son,
my brother and Savior, Jesus. Amen

September 17, 1977
Fleeting Moments of Loneliness

Fleeting moments of loneliness,
remembering how things once were
and may yet be, but are not now.
Memories carefully tucked away,
to bring melancholy tears on silent nights...
memories of hand holding
and toe-touching under sheets.
Memories of a strong arm
around my waist in the midnight hours.
Memories of two so different
becoming one, and even being blessed by it.
And You were there, Lord,
in my womanly fullness,
You were there.
And now I freely cry in my solidarity,
and You're here Lord.
You're here.
I have been strong.
I haven't given in to my emptiness yet,

But I do now.

Jesus, fill my void with You and Your love.

Take this empty feeling and use it for Your glory.

You said it is not good for man to be alone.

You said for this cause

shall a man leave his parents

and the two shall become one flesh.

I have become one flesh

and my flesh is divided.

Restore our wholeness.

Soon, Lord, very soon.

I need my husband.

My children need their daddy.

We all need You!

Thank you, Jesus!

September 20, 1977
Cleansed by my Tears

Lord, I thank You for loving me
and accepting me as Your child.
I cried tonight, Lord, because of my imperfection
and my insecurity within myself.
I wept tears of penitential cleansing
because I know I'm so far
from what You would have me to be.
But now, Lord, that I've admitted my shortcomings,
You've already renewed my strength.
I still don't understand
why You should be so patient
and persistent with me,
but I accept Your acceptance.
Thank you, Lord, for taking me...
breaking me... remaking me.
Do with me what You will.
Take me, Lord! I'm Yours!!!

September 27, 1977
Evening Gone Awry!

Hello, Lord.
Its evening again,
I know I sound like a replay
for thinking and watching, just relaxing.
Wait a minute, Lord... I take that back!
Little fingers are trying to shanghai my pen and
style my hair---
my miniature grandpa just met me face-to-face to
ask me to mow our grass—
the baby's heading into the two-foot-high weeds
to play with the water faucet
and firstborn son just made a beeline
to his room unexplainedly!!!
Momma! Mamma!!! Mama!!!
Excuse me, Lord!
Here's a raincheck on my letter!
Thanks. Amen!

October 4, 1977
The Sacrifice of a Smile

Lord, I learned something today.

By your grace,

I learned that a smile can be a sacrifice.

A sacrifice pure and holy

and pleasing to You

if done for Your glory,

not for a melancholy nicety.

I wanted to cry.

I wanted to scream out

"My world is falling apart!"

But I didn't.

I whispered a prayer to You, Jesus, And

You answered.

You wiped away my tears...

You gave me back my smile...

You reassured me

that You ARE in control!

And even as I answered the phones,

I let my voice smile.

No one knew what was going on inside of me

Except You,

And I offered that smile

as a sacrifice of praise.

And You, Lord, restored my peace.

I love You, Lord.

Thank You for caring for me

As Your child.

(This happened on the third day when I took my toddler to a babysitter after I had started working a temporary job as a telephone operator. He had clung to me the first 2 days and I felt sad. The third day, he flew to her arms and turned his back on me as if I were betraying him. The pain went straight to my heart, but I had to go to work as if nothing had happened. It was indeed a sacrifice for me to smile, but I gave the pain to Jesus.)

October 15, 1977
Metamorphosis

Can a butterfly go back to its cocoon
once its wings have tasted freedom?
Can a chick return to its shell
once its feathers have dried
and its learned to scratch?
Can a flower
become an enclosed bud once more
after it has blossomed forth?
I don't think so, Lord,
And I don't like I could ever go back
to being the "me" I was not so long ago.
I've grown, Lord. I've changed.
And You are the Master workman
shaping and molding my life,
carving ever so carefully the little
details You want perfected in me.
I was setting up like slip for greenware
for the past few years.
You let me go through many things

till my spirit reached the right consistency.
And now, Lord, You've begun a working me
that I will not let man destroy.
Be what I was?
NO! not ever again!!!
Be what You would have me to be?
Yes, Lord, day by day.
Take me, I'm Yours!!! Amen!

November 5, 1977
Praying for my Husband

Lord, tonight I pray for my husband.
You have seen fit to delay our divorce, Lord.
You've let me continue in my separate way.
You've opened doors for me
that I could not have entered as his wife.
I don't understand, Lord.
You're giving me responsibilities and new
horizons that he would not let his "Mrs." enter.
But You are keeping me as his "Mrs."
So I pray for him, Lord.
May Your work be completed speedily.
May he find Your peace soon, even this night.
May he accept Your love and forgiveness
May he give his love and forgiveness to others.
May he be Your evangelist
to all those unsaved
people in his family.
May his rebirth glorify You in the highest.
May he recognize the work You've done in me.

May his love for me be renewed
And mine, in turn, for him.
May Your powers of inner healing
flow through both of us
To use the nightmare memories
for positive actions
and not painful thoughts.
May we work together to glorify You
And rear our children in the
admonition And knowledge of you.
Thank you, Jesus! Amen!!

December 1, 1977
Suppressing Loneliness

Dear Lord,
The loneliness in me clicked back on
tonight With that certain phone call.
Lord, I've suppressed my void,
But tonight, I was actually tempted
To say 'yes', I'll go.
Lord, forgive my self-pities.
Forgive me my desire for companionship.
Forgive me, Lord,
for wanting to pretend
things are not what they are.
Help me keep my eyes on You
and not on people.
Praise You, Jesus, for being sufficient.
Thank you, Lord, for Your love.
Amen!

December 27, 1977
Breakthrough?

Well, Lord,
I feel like we're on the verge of a breakthrough.
Time has healed some wounds quite nicely,
and I believe with some encouragement,
I could learn to love my husband all over again.
Yes, there are a few scars left,
because the total healing process is not done.
But I don't feel hostile anymore, and that's a start.
Lord, we are still worlds apart,
we are still on different wave lengths.
But he called the other night and we talked.
Maybe my loneliness has caught up with me and
he is still the legitimate answer.
But maybe we both realize
we can have a new beginning through You.
So, Lord, now I pray that if this be Your doing,
and if I be out of step with Your timing, implant the
self-dissatisfaction all over again.
Thanks, Lord Jesus. I'm trusting You.
Amen.

Unknown date, 1977
A New Game

We started a new game today
And it was a challenge for all of us.
We got into the play early
as I delivered my kids and me
to our positions.
The oldest went to grandma's house
so she could take him to school.
I delivered the in-between ones to their
schools before I went to my job.
Then, I rushed to take
my baby to the sitter,
And I made it to work
with 2 seconds to spare.
Bless you, Jesus!
Second quarter was a breeze,
And I made morning to midday,
With modified fumbles.
Half time at lunch was a needed intermission.
Second half was smooth sailing.

Thank you, precious Jesus.
Then came the emotional letdown.
at day's end after the game.
Not a defeated let down...
Just pent-up energy needing to drain, Almost.
My tear ducts leaked,
but they didn't cry.
Satan was my opponent
and he wasn't satisfied.
He tried putting fever on my little girl and rain in the clouds.
The fever left.
Then the night stars shone through.
And now, I can lay back and unwind.
Listen to the quiet of the night
Without the cheering team egging me on
For touchdowns on their bottom sides,
Watch their intermission
While their healthy bodies rest so peacefully.
I contemplate what You, "Coach,"
are trying to make out of me

and teach me in this phase of life.
Yes, Lord, I may be alone,
but I'm certainly not on my own.
Thank you for choosing me
to be on Your winning team.
Yaaaaa! Christians!!!
Amen! Amen!

February 25, 1978
Satellite

Dear Poppa God,
I'm lonely and I'm reluctant to admit it.
I feel like a satellite,
revolving off by myself somewhere,
doing what I was created to do,
but somehow feeling very incomplete.
Lord, I long for a one-on-one relationship,
but in You and through You.
But Lord, the emptiness seems so great at times.
Tonight, in our prayers,
I felt an invisible hug coming from You to me,
I felt Your presence and I felt reassured.
Somehow, I had gotten my eyes onto the people
who seemingly neglect me
instead of keeping them on the Lord,
who never lets me down.
Thank you, Jesus! I love You!!! Amen!

November 2, 1978 9:30pm Uptight!

Hey, God!
I was feeling pretty uptight while ago.
just sort of realized where I was a year ago,
and I see where am now,
and I got a little overwhelmed, actually.
I felt like You didn't know what you were doing,
Giving me this much responsibility.
After all, what's a woman with four kids,
And no husband
Doing in a job that's built
for a career minded person?
It just doesn't make sense.
But then, God,
I realized that You are still Lord,
no matter how inadequate I feel.
And I have made You Lord of my life,
so that makes You Lord of my inadequacies, too.
Okay, Lord, You win!

I'm going to keep trusting You,
no matter how my mind tells me things are
going. I'm going to keep trusting,
no matter how circumstances
tell me things are going.
And no matter how many times
I hit the wrong keys,
I'm going to keep trusting
That the eventual outcome is going to be
just as You planned.
Forgive my doubts, Lord.
Bless me, Lord.
I come before You
in my total nothingness,
Depending totally on You
for whatever good
may come from my efforts.
Strengthen me, Lord.
Keep me mindful
of living one day at a time,
minute by minute.
Help me to see You
in everyone I come in contact with.

Help me to care as You would care

for those in sorrow

and help me to encourage

those who need encouraging.

Keep me mindful of my beginnings

so that I never pretend to

be what I am not.

Thank you, Lord, for loving me and caring.

And thank You, Lord, for continuing

to keep Your shield around me

in spite of myself.

Praise you, Lord, and come soon!!!

Maranatha!

Amen!

November, 1978
Memories

Ten years ago...
Memories dart back and forth
like starlings diving for mosquitos
Or frogs zapping flies.
I remember senior year,
Supposedly the highlight of high school. No
one told my social life that.
Homecoming... Christmas parties.....
Valentines... the prom...
Somehow, I was the everblooming wall
flower, a perennial favorite at hen parties
and volunteer labor affairs.
A good old girl, I suppose,
but uncomfortably unapproachable.
Had an image to live up to.
The prom found me and several others
from the garden of late bloomers
sharing our woes
of not being invited to the gala affair.

Jovial desperation set in,
and so, to keep from crying,
I caught a frog and labelled him for all to see,
"Kiss me quick--- I may be a prince in disguise!"
Well, it didn't work... no one was that desperate,
but the laughter didn't stop the hurt.
Writing became a way of escape and release.
And who better to write to
than this Person we call God?
I mean, after all, if anyone should be able to
help, He should.
So began a reassuring relationship
when I needed someone to talk to,
Me and God would get together
and peace flowed like a river,
Beginning turbulently at times,
but always ending up in restful waters.
My Father cared.

August 1, 1979
Your Wandering Child

Dear Lord,
Your wandering child wants to come
home... to Your presence.
Lord, I've missed fellowship with You.
I've slacked off,
I've made excuses,
I've been taking things
back into my own hands.
Lord, You've been so good to me,
in spite of myself.
You've increased my finances.
You've given me favor.
You've taken care of every need I could
have. You 've given us energy
and you've given us so much
our cup runneth over.
Lord, I miss You!
I know You've been with me,
But I'm not so sure I've been with you.

I feel like I'm falling apart on the inside
And I know it's not physical.
Lord, renew Your Spirit within me,
I can't make it on my own.
and I can't make it with any other person.
I do need You!
I ask Your forgiveness.
Thank You, Lord.
I love You

Broken Heart Mender
(Probably written in 1979)

I remember, Lord,
when I gave my heart away.
I knew it was fragile and I knew it could be
broken, but I was in "love,"
and my heart was all I had to give.
Things were okay for a while,
but soon some hairline fractures appeared.
My heart had a few nicks
and chips along the way
but it wasn't mine anymore
because I had given it away.
So I smiled and continued to live
without a heart of my own.
Eventually, Lord, my "love" decided
he didn't want my heart anymore,
So he gave it back to me,
hairline fractures and all.
I didn't want it back,
So I refused to accept it.

Then, to make sure he didn't get it back at all,
he took it and broke it into a million pieces.
And I was left without a love, without a heart.
How do you mend a broken heart?
You showed me in Your Word.
Your Balm of Gilead soaked into my broken
spirit and began restoring the broken pieces.
Your comforter came to me
and gave me hope for a future.
Piece by piece, chip by chip,
You put back the pieces of the puzzle of my
life and gave me new life in You.
You, Lord, mended my broken heart.
And if I should ever fall in love again,
I won't give my heart away
because my heart belongs to You.
You are the Broken Heart Mender.
Maranatha, my Lord.
Amen!

Part 2
Other
Reflections On
Life
In Prose
Song,
And Poetry

The Miracle from the Tithe

I was a young mother with four lively young 'uns in the early "70's when I first learned of the blessings of tithing. But I had a problem and it would take a miracle from God Himself for me to be able to tithe. You see, although I was a new believer in the Lord Jesus Christ, I was also in a marriage that was full of strife and discord and a severe lack of finances. Nonetheless, I heard about tithing on Christian radio, found the Biblical support for it, and wanted to do my part as a believer. All I needed to do was do it. But how? My husband rarely gave me any grocery money, much less money to do anything else with, so, when he gave me $40 for groceries one day in '76, I was so excited that I spent it all on groceries and forgot to keep out the tithe. Now I had to figure out how to make things right, so I started mulling the problem over.

My solution turned out to be quite simple... tithe on the groceries. I contacted a friend and asked her to be my private investigator to find someone with a need. Marleah did as asked and came up with the name of a family who had met hard times financially and had 2 or 3 kids and one on the way (I think that is what happened). They were without groceries till their next pay check and I believed God wanted to use me to bless them. Excitedly, I started grabbing from my groceries and packing in things I thought would bless them... hamburger meat, bread, sugar, eggs, etcetera, until I had filled not one, but two bags, much more than 10% of my purchase. Then I asked Marleah to be my go-between, to deliver the goods to them, but not let them know who their benefactor was. Marleah was true to her word and I felt like I had not let the Lord down after all.

I forgot about the matter for several months and then, out of the blue, the couple contacted me. As it turned out, they were getting ready to move and could not take everything with them. Would I be offended if they gave me what was left in their pantry? By this time, they were back on their feet, but my marriage had totally fallen apart and I was having to move closer to my parents, so I readily accepted their offer. Laughingly and rejoicing over God's goodness, I shared with them how the Lord had used me in their lives a few months before and now I was receiving their overflow. As I loaded and unloaded their items, I was shocked to find just how much over flow.... between food, clothing, and odds and ends of furniture, toys, and stuff, the total value of everything was well over $200! Not bad for returns on a $4 tithe!!! No one can tell me you can't out-give God!

Jesus Protected Us in Apartment 77

I was a mother of 4 under the age of 7, recently divorced, and living in government housing. Our apartment number was 77, a number I associated with God and His love. Our church in Wharton, Texas, had been holding a revival with Evangelist Gary Wood and after the last Saturday night service, I was pumped and full of the Word.

That night after my kids and I got back to our 2-story apartment, we ended up playing musical beds—- my oldest son was in my bed, my 4-year-old daughter was in his bed, two other boys were in other beds, and I was in my daughter's bed. We were all sleeping peacefully, but about 2 in the morning, I awoke to find a tall figure standing by my bed (actually, my daughter's bed because of our rearranged sleeping arrangements.) Although I kept my cool, I immediately questioned him about how he had gotten in and why he was there.

It was as though the Hand of God drew me out of bed and wrapped my sheet around me, then tied an invisible rope around the intruder's neck and led him down stairs to the front door. His story was that he had gotten in through the bedroom window and he came to get something that my son had supposedly gotten from his nephew. He couldn't explain why he had to break in through an upstairs window in the middle of the night to take care of something that could easily be handled in the daylight.

As I followed him down the stairs, I started talking to him about Jesus and how He was in charge of our lives and wanted to be in charge of his, too. He stood just inside the door for a long time, probably 10-15 minutes, and I carried on a one-sided conversation the whole time. At one point, I prayed audibly in tongues. This must have spooked him, because he instantly asked me, "What did you say, Lady?"

I explained that he had me so upset that I didn't know how to pray, so I was praying in a language that God would understand. Surprisingly, he didn't run and he stayed put long enough for me to invite him to church the next day. He agreed, but didn't show up when it was time to go.

After he left, then I thought of all the scenarios that COULD have happened... had my daughter been in her bed instead of me being there... If he had a weapon or intentions to hurt any of us... If he had tried to overpower me and take advantage of me as a single female...if he had wanted to hurt any of my children, especially my little girl... if he had tried to help himself to what few valuables we possessed. Thanks be to our Heavenly Father and Lord Jesus, none of those things took place.

It was then that I checked the windows and found out that he had indeed climbed on top of a fence in order to get in through the window. I went all through the rooms and locked the windows that I had never thought about locking before. I called the police after the fact to let them know there had been a break in. When they came to check on us, they assured me that they would be making rounds in our complex during the night to ensure our safety. Finally, I gave myself permission to have a crying jag. It was a long time before I was able to go back to sleep.

I shared this testimony with Brother Woods and

the congregation the next day at church and I believe it helped to build faith in others. I learned new tricks for protection, especially using dowel sticks slanted sideways above the windows to keep them from opening. My children's safety became my main concern and they rarely played outside with the neighbors.

Although the government housing was a blessing, I never expected the problems that came from living there. However, God uses all kinds of things to teach His children lessons and the lesson I learned in Meadows Apartment #77 was that God looks out for His children and He has it all under control.

Kicked off Welfare to Buy a House

I gathered my dignity as I left the realtor's office with his words ringing in my ears.... "There's no way a woman in your situation can buy a home. You might as well forget it!"

Humanly speaking, it was true, but I wasn't depending on humans... I was depending on God and I knew He would make a way. My situation was precarious, to say the least. A newly divorced young mother with four children under the age of six, living in government housing and receiving food stamps, working a low paying job and paying babysitters for child care. Yes, it did look bleak, but I knew God was working for my good and I proceeded to act like it.

My children and I had lived in government subsidized apartment for almost two years and life there was getting scary. Fear kept my young ones from playing outside. Neighbors were as nervous as we were because of recent shootings that had taken place. One night, I found an intruder standing by my bedside, supposedly looking for my young son whom he said had borrowed his brother's wristwatch. I shuddered to think that I was in my daughter's bed that night and what would have happened had she been where she was supposed to be instead of playing musical beds. Yes, it was definitely time to move on.

My first step of faith was to open a savings account, announcing to the Lord that this was the seed for the home that I knew He was going to help me buy. Once upon a time, I had lent a friend $200 and now, several months later, he repaid the loan. That was the beginning of my nest egg. My confession was continually in my mouth and in my mind... "God is going to help me buy a house."

Well, since I was going to buy a house, I acted like it. After the first. realtor blew me off, I looked for another one. This time, I was treated with respect and hope. Sam couldn't help me himself, so he introduced me to Barbara, who took me under her wing. I explained my family situation, my work obligations, my lack of finances, and my faith that God was in charge. Rather than laugh at my dreams, she sought to help me fulfill them.

It was easy to see that Barbara took me seriously. She began searching their listings, leaving no possibility unchecked. Finally, she came up with a suggestion... a 65 by 12-foot mobile home, with three bedrooms, and one and a half bathrooms, sitting on a fifty by a hundred-and fifty-foot lot in a quiet neighborhood. If I remember correctly, it was about $16,000. And for the low-down payment of only about 25%, the property could be mine! Never mind the fact that I had less than $1,000 and not many prospects for achieving $4,000. Or that I had no one to turn to except God. I believed in my heart that this was the home God had in store for me. All of this took place in January and I put my faith in action, full speed ahead.

My faith was put to the test in many ways but I continued believing. Shortly after I started the savings account, I received a letter from Uncle Sam stating that I no longer qualified for welfare because I had received two consecutive child support payments and that put me in the category of being an independent woman. What they didn't acknowledge was that each payment was only $100 and that it had gotten caught up in the "system", so I had not received it. To top that off, my four-year-old daughter became very sick and since we were no longer on welfare, I didn't know how I was going to pay for the doctor. But I was tenacious in believing God would not abandon me and I continued my quest. When you really step out in faith, things will start to happen. My tax return was going to bring in about $800, so that would take a chunk. A local congressman got involved in the fight to release my child support from the red tape of bureaucracy, so that brought forth another $200 (the only child support I ever received). I received a pay increase on the job and started receiving some commissions, so that added to my nest egg. A little here, a little there, a little from someplace else, the money started adding up, but it still was not even close to the $4,000 I needed. Then God stepped in...

Unexpectedly, Barbara had taken my case to heart. She called me one evening to ask me a question. "There is a group of people who would like to talk to you about your house. Do you think you could meet with them Sunday night?"

"Sure," I replied. "Just tell me when and where."

Butterflies in my stomach worked overtime between that phone call and our scheduled meeting at the Methodist Church. Five couples were assembled and Barbara was there as a representative of a women's civic organization. Then the inquisition began...

"Tell us about yourself."
"Tell us about your kids and family."
"Why do you want to move?"
"What are your plans for the future?"

"Why should we make a decision to help you?"

"How do you plan to make your payments?"

Various other questions rolled my way before the group went into a closed conference. After all was said and done, each couple agreed to give me $265 toward the down payment, plus the benevolent fund of their church contributed some, as did the Women's Service League. The previous homeowners decided to let me take a side note with them for part of the closing costs. My heart was racing and my tears were flowing when I realized my dream to own a home had just been made possible.

My stoical Dad could not fathom that perfect strangers could reach out to help someone in need like me. What he didn't realize was that Someone Greater than they had moved them into action. God had delivered more than I could have hoped or even dreamed. From start to finish, my journey of faith took about two months, including the encounter with the original realtor. My young ones and I moved into that haven about March 18, 1979, and our payments were $173 a month, a sum I could easily handle, With God's help, I was never late or in jeopardy of losing our dream home.

Now, I admit, a trailer isn't exactly Taj Mahal, but when you're a young mother looking out for your brood, a trailer can be a Haven of Rest. Since that time, I have had many blessings in my life that have solidified my faith even more, But no matter how much time goes by, I will never forget the sheer joy and happiness that those people brought to my life by their act of love. Although we have all gone on to greater and grander homes since then, I will never forget how God kicked us off welfare to buy us a home.

Using the Foolish to Confound the Wise

Life is full of surprises and the things that a person expects to happen don't always happen. One of the most surprising things I've found in life is that God uses foolish things (like me) to confound the wise (like people who are much better qualified.) I found this out quite a few years ago in a most amazing way. Then it happened several more times and God is not finished with me yet. One of the standout times was when I returned to the work world after separation and divorce and had four little ones under the age of 6 to care for.

Somehow, with God as my guide, I ended up working at our local radio station...KANI Country Radio, 1500 on your AM dial. I started small by pre-recording and reading bedtime stories. I didn't get paid for that service, but I did get my foot in the door. After a few weeks, I was asked if I would like to sell ads on commission. I was comfortable dealing with people for the most part, so I accepted their offer. It wasn't long after that that Stan, the newsman, quit and I was offered his position with the benefit of a regular salary. I accepted the job with fear and trepidation and became the number one (and only) news reporter for our little country station, It was the first part of September and I think I started the next day.

My first day on the air was disastrous! One of the Dj's did the morning news till I got situated. Midday news was my debut and it was unforgettable! As I sat behind the announcer's mike, reading the news itself was fairly easy. Rip and read is what it was called... pulling news stories off the Associated Press wire.

When it came time for the stock market report, I did fine until I got to the symbol- PU for public utilities, All I could see was "P-U" and I started imagining people paying for something that smelled really bad. I laughed so hard the guy at the control desk had to go to a commercial... and then another... and probably a third by the time I was composed enough to continue. Somehow, I muddled through and reminded myself to be prepared for the next time I reported.

Mornings were a challenge because I still had to get my kids to school and day care. We finally compromised by allowing me to read news remotely from home and the DJ would put my voice on the air with the news stories. We lived in a 3-bedroom government subsidized 2 story apartment at that time, so I set up my "office" in the downstairs closet under the stairs. Pride filled my heart as I hooked up all the right connections and started my report. I made it through the first couple of stories before I thought the DJ was talking to me. "Huh, what did you say? What do you want? I can't hear you!" I repeated these lines over and over until I realized it was my toddler coming downstairs, wanting to know what we were having for breakfast! The DJ once again switched to commercials until the problem was taken care of. Another infamous flub in my stunning career as a reporter.

It took a while, but we eventually figured out how to make this work. I would record my news on a cassette tape early in the morning. The morning disc jockey would stop by my apartment and pick it up on his way to work. Using this system, I was able to report the news and still get my children taken care of before I actually reported to work. It was a crazy way to do things, but it worked for us. Once I got into the swing of things, it was fairly smooth sailing. Every morning started with phone calls to the local DPS (Department of Public Safety) to find out what accidents had happened in the last 24 hours. Sometimes the notes were full, sometimes, not so much. Sometimes they gave me stories from around the state. Being the thorough reporter I was, I called each newsworthy story to the AP.

After a few weeks, I didn't even have to say my name. Their news desk would hear my voice and automatically ask, "What do you have for us today, Liz?" Every time they printed one of my news articles, they gave me the by-line. Even when the story was something that I had no first-hand knowledge of, I was given credit and the stories spread across the state. One time I got a call from the Jacksonville, Texas, radio station, wanting me to give the details of one of the wrecks I reported on. This was really weird, especially since the accident happened in their neck of the world. There's a few hundred miles distance between our stations and I tried to explain this to the caller, but to no avail. Since I was the one who broke the story, they wanted me to be the one who read it on air.

Once, I talked my boss into paying for me to attend a news reporter's conference in Beaumont. When I signed in, some people were looking over my shoulder and noticed my signature. "Oh," they said, "you're the one sending all those stories to the AP!" I didn't realize I had gained any notoriety by doing my job. But the best payoff was yet to come.

On the morning of November 10, 1978, I came back to the office after running my rounds, and everyone stood and clapped as I entered the room. I took a bow as I thanked them and gave them a quizzical look. "You don't know what happened, do you?" Billie asked me. "Well, no, not really," I replied. "What did happen?" "Here, read this," she said.

She had ripped a page off the newswire that stated our station, KANI, had been named the top Associated Press news station for the month of October, my second month of news reporting. I was told later that many journalists had sought that prize for years but to no avail. Here I didn't even know there was a prize and had put others to shame.

This job lasted for a season, but it was long enough to garner a regular salary and switch back to sales with higher commissions. Although I had few marketable skills, I ended up making over $22,000 that year. After all the mistakes and comedies of errors, God really did choose to use the foolish to confound the wise.

Jeremiah 29:11 I know the plans I have for you, plans to prosper you and not to harm you, plans for a hope and a future.

Keep on Trucking!

If someone would have told me fifty years ago all the twists and turns my life would take, I would have said, "No, obviously you have me mixed up with someone else!" But here I am, a lot older and hopefully a lot wiser, and I can tell you for sure my life has been like a roller coaster ride, with God in total control.

There was a time when our family hit an unexpected hard patch. My children were still in school and I hadn't started back to college yet. Beverly Irish, a friend of mine that I knew because of KANI Radio, had a frozen food delivery service and needed extra help. I was desperate enough to accept the challenge. With a little training and a lot of bravado, I began working for Bi-Quality Foods.

A few months after I began the job, Beverly decided to move out of state and offered the business to me. She made it so that I could take over payments on the truck (I always compared it to a Frito Lay delivery van). Her account list included many cities in south east Texas, including Wharton, Boling, Newgulf, Columbus, Eagle Lake, Schulenburg, Weimar, Wallis, and Garwood.

One of the first things I had to do was make arrangements for the two freezers on the truck to be plugged in while resting at home. Another problem I had to tackle was purchasing food from the restaurant supplier Sysco. Repackaging the food was a precise operation, needing a good scale, plastic gloves, and lots of Ziploc bags.

Once I started ordering food, I learned to do something I never had to do before --- write checks for hundreds of dollars at a time to pay for the product. I had to depend on selling enough food really quick in order to cover the checks I had written before they came back to be paid at the bank.

Sysco Foods out of Houston usually delivered once a week, but they weren't my only supplier. Occasionally we had to pick up products from other companies. There were times we went to Sam's stores on the southwest side of Houston. Going to Matagorda in the van to get breaded shrimp and crab rolls was easy compared to the trips we made to San Antonio to get supplies of Manhattan Palletas. That was a harrowing experience, to say the least!

This was 30 years ago, before seatbelts were legally required. There was only one installed seat for the driver and we put a chair on the passenger side for whoever would ride shotgun. There were problems with the side mirrors and no inside rear-view mirror, so driving on the freeways of San Antonio was testing God's grace. Sliding in and out of traffic was terrifying! Thankfulness filled our hearts when we arrived at our destination and even more so when we arrived home. Thank God for my son Patrick who was quite frequently my designated driver on this eight-hour trip there and back.

We had a gas generator inside the truck but it wasn't very efficient. It was noisy, added heat to the inside, and it was smelly, but we had to try to keep the electricity going. There was no insulation on the top of the truck, so I frequently felt that my brain was being cooked. It took a lot of effort to open and close both side doors--- so much so that I developed tendonitis and carpal tunnel syndrome for a season. Sometimes I wondered if the benefits outweighed the complications.

Although there were difficulties and my family still qualified for food stamps, we ate well during that time. My family loved the precooked chicken fajitas and hamburger patties, but especially fried cheese sticks, cream cheese jalapeños, and personal pan pizzas. I made sure we did not deplete our stock. No one complained when I brought home leftovers from holding a food show. (This was an effort to advertise the products to influence more people to become customers.)

We didn't have a car back then, so the Bi-Quality van was our family transportation on many trips to town. Once, when we were going to see in-laws in Gonzales, we had a blowout on one of the back-country roads. The noise scared the heck out of our kids, who were sleeping on a mattress in the back of the truck, We weren't too far from one of my cousins, so his son Daryl came to help us out.

Another time, we loaded up our kids and family dog Balkie for a short vacation trip to Rockport. We paid a few dollars extra to plug in to their electricity and even sold a little bit of food to people in Rockport so we could count our stay as a business trip.

Looking back, I realize how dependent we were on that truck and the business. So many of the things I've been involved in lasted for a season, including my ownership of Bi Quality Foods. I remember driving down Highway 71 from El Campo to Garwood, praying and asking God what He wanted me to do with my life. After all, I was nearing 40 and it looked like I was getting nowhere fast. His Spirit spoke to me gently and authoritatively, "You're doing it!" So I kept on trucking.

It wasn't too long after that that I applied to finish my education. After I finally started back to college, there were times that I had to take that van to get me to class at University of Houston in Victoria. It wasn't my favorite means of transportation but it got me where I was going.

After I got my teaching degree, I still had to depend on the truck for transportation to Newgulf. I can't remember now if it was my first or second year of teaching that it got to be too much, so, with Beverly's permission, I sold the truck and disbanded the business. With a thankful heart and lots of memories, I closed that chapter of my life.

I met so many wonderful people during this time that I looked forward to visiting with them as much as I enjoyed selling wonderful products. I could start giving names, but I know I would leave someone out, so I'll stop here.

Although it was a challenging time, we made it through with perseverance and consistent faith in the God of the Universe. Because of this experience, I grew in my ability to walk by faith and not by sight. And, I hope in the process, that He was glorified.

I Remember Going Back to College

We were both middle aged matrons with families to care for and little or no income to speak of. Both of us were friends from as far back as high school in the '60's, and both of us attended Wharton County Junior College many moons ago. Both of us were frustrated with the lack of worldly goods in our lives and the need to use food stamps to get by. And then, seemingly out of the blue, my friend Faye got a harebrained idea. "Liz," she said, "I'm going back to college. Why don't you come, too?"

With five kids at home, a husband with little income, and a food delivery business that was getting nowhere fast, I laughed at the improbability of it all. But then, the words of my college professor Dr. C.P. Williams came back to haunt me. He, too, had cajoled me to complete my degree. "But Dr. Williams," I whined, "I'm 38 years old and it's been 17 years since I finished WCJC!"

He smiled as he asked, "How old will you be if you do go back to college and get your certification?"

Weakly, I replied, "Forty-one."

"And," he continued, "How old will you be if you DON'T go back?" Since time was going to pass either way, it looked like I might as well do something productive to help improve our situation in life.

So, after immense prayer and soul searching, I was a student again, juggling classes and car pools to UH-Victoria and family obligations in Wharton. God must have helped me in my plans the first time around because all but seven of my 126 credits from the early '70's transferred after the interim. What surprised me was how many other middle-aged mommas and men were also making midlife career changes by going back to school. Although there were many young people enrolled, it seemed that there were just as many of us who were young at heart.

Testing at all the steps along the way was a real night mare... placement tests, TASP tests, class tests, semester exams, and, finally, ExCet tests. My poor family suffered as their loving, mild mannered mother became a screaming, temperamental tyrant when it came time to do special reports for classes or to meet certain deadlines for individual teachers. Finding a compatible carpool was another challenge that weighed heavily in choosing courses each new semester. Although I qualified for Pell grants and financial aid along the way, I still had to keep up my business and other obligations.

Someone was kind enough to lend me an electric typewriter for my college work. (this was before the widespread use of computers.) With God's help and abundant grace, I completed my work in about two and a half years. In spite of the struggle and inconvenience, I am so glad that accepted the challenge. I used to feel very guilty because I had received many scholarships when I graduated high school in 1969, but didn't follow through on completing my college program. Because of God's help, I believe I have been able to justify and honor the faith that my benefactors had in me, albeit on a delayed basis. Resuming my education was one of the hardest decisions I have ever made, but one that brings me great pride. Although I considered myself late bloomer, I am glad to say that I did bloom and brought forth fruit with each and every new school year that I taught.

Detoured to Israel by Way of Junior High

Once upon a time over 30 year ago, I had a dream of visiting the country of Israel. I scrimped and saved for almost a year in order to make the trip with the Women's Aglow organization, and just days before it was time to turn in the final fees, I was about $200 short. I was heartbroken as I cancelled out, thinking how close I had come to a dream of a lifetime. Life went on and somehow, I tucked that dream in the back of my mind. Maybe I would go to Israel when it came time to go to the New Jerusalem in the next life. After all, I had a new husband and four young children from a previous marriage, so what was I thinking that I could leave on a trip like that, even if I could have afforded it... Fast forward to 2006. I had gone back to college and was now a junior high teacher, something I had never imagined for myself. My first year in junior high ten years earlier was a nightmare, and I tried unsuccessfully to relocate. Every time I lost out on a new job possibility, it was like God telling me, "Be still... I've got you here for a reason." After that first year, I learned to adapt because I realized the kids weren't going to change. Life became more bearable when I accepted that fact.

One of the things I taught as a junior high language arts teacher was literature concerning the Holocaust. Because of that curriculum, I became passionate in teaching it and learning more about it. Eventually, I met Helen Colin, a Holocaust survivor from Poland who lived in Houston. (That's another story in itself.) After several years of knowing her, she asked me how I would like to go on a study trip to Poland and Israel in order to learn more about the Holocaust. That was in 2005.

The program Mrs. Colin was talking about was the Teachers' Summer Seminar on the Holocaust and Jewish resistance, sponsored by the National Jewish Labor League for teachers to participate in the educational travel experience. My travel expenses would be paid by the group of Holocaust survivors in Houston. The participants were to spend time in Poland visiting various Holocaust sites followed by a trip to Israel. Wow! I would have never expected anything like that when I started teaching fourteen years earlier! Of course, my answer was Yes! Yes! Yes! Immediately, I looked into the needed paperwork and did all that was required to be accepted. In spite of all my effort, it was too late for the program that year, but it was in plenty time to get it in the works for 2006 Meticulously, I requested character references and wrote pages and pages of information explaining why I thought I was worthy of the privilege and what I expected to learn. After all was said and done, I waited...and waited...and waited. Then I received the word from their New York headquarters...the first miracle... I was accepted! Now began the real work: passports and preparation for what was supposed to be a ten-day trip. July came and I ventured to New York to meet up with the rest of the group. I shared those memories with a daily blog in the *Victoria Advocate*, so I won't go into all those details now. We spent several days in Poland, then were ready to make the journey the rest of the way to Israel. Very unexpectedly, our plans were deflated like a balloon that was blown up and let go...missiles were being shot in Nahariya, the very city we were to go to and some of them landed on the street in front of the hotel that we were going to stay in. as you can imagine, we were in a daze.

Most of us couldn't believe the way our trip was ending. Those of us who had cell phones scrambled to make calls to loved ones and tell them. Those without phones waited frantically to borrow the phones for themselves. We tried to encourage each other that maybe next year would be our year, the completion of our dream, But to be honest, it seemed impossible. I had lost my second trip to visit the land of my Lord.   And then another miracle happened...we received notification that we would be able to join the 2007 seminar group when they went to.... you guessed it.... Israel! My dream of walking where Jesus walked was going to happen and I couldn't have been happier.

Because of this incredible experience in Poland and Israel, I had more firsthand knowledge of that period in History and was able to help Mrs. Colin write her autobiography, **My Dream of Freedom, From Holocaust to my Beloved America**, which came out in 2013. (It's available on Amazon or from the Holocaust Museum in Houston for less than $10.)

Although she passed away at 93 years old in 2016, she continued to share her story whenever she was physically able. By the way, I forgot to mention that when we met, we discovered that my Dad, John Dettling of Wharton, Texas, had helped to liberate Dachau, the camp her husband had been interred in. That was the tie that brought our families together permanently. She became my adopted Jewish mother. Yes, I did get to visit Israel and it was a trip I will never forget. All along the way, I was aware of God's hand working things out for my good.

It took the detour I never expected- being a junior high teacher- for it to come to pass. This is just more proof that our ways are not God's way and all things work together for good to those who love God, to those who are the called according to His purpose.

Jeremiah 29:11
New King James Version (NKJV)

For I know the thoughts that I think toward you, says the LORD, thoughts of peace and not of evil, to give you a future and a hope.

How I Met Helen Colin

I became interested in Holocaust studies in 1996 when I first started teaching at Bay City Junior High. *Devil's Arithmetic* was on another teacher's agenda, so I followed her lead. Up until that time, I'm not sure that I had even heard the word "holocaust" and I certainly did not realize what it involved. Because of that original experience, I can honestly say I'm not who I used to be and I have become passionate about teaching the lessons of the Holocaust so this generation of adolescents may become witnesses to future generations.

Two years later, I insisted that my husband accompany me to the Holocaust Museum in Houston so that I could see for myself just what kinds of things took place. I was dumbfounded to see what great extent the NAZI's went to to torture the Jews. An idea began burning inside me to bring our students for a field trip so that they, too, might gain an appreciation for this time in History. It took a bit of coaxing to get our principal to agree, but we finally succeeded in arranging a trip.

That year was when I heard Walter Kase's story for the first time. As a teenager, he was a captive in the Mauthausen camp. After liberation, he was able to relocate to the Houston, Texas, area. When he finished telling about his liberation, my heart started pounding as he talked about the American tank driver who got out of his tank, talked to him about the horrors he was seeing, and then gave him a Hershey's chocolate with almonds in it.

My Dad, John Dettling of Wharton, Texas, had told that same story to us as we were growing up, but in his version, he was the driver! When I was a child, it was just a story without much meaning, but now it became as real to me as the air I was breathing! I sobbed and sobbed as I retold Dad's share of the story to Walter and the students in the room.

I ended up writing a letter to Mr. Kase and the museum describing that unique relationship. It was the following year when Dad received an invitation from the museum to share his war stories for the archives as. one of the liberators. He did go to have that interview and his fascinating stories are preserved for future generations. That event led to Dad and Mom being invited the following year to the special banquet to honor the liberators and I certainly wished I could attend with them, but tickets were a mere $500 each. There was no way we could afford that type of money, but something else happened to spark an idea and make it possible, My younger sister Helen and her husband Mark Monfrey lived in Dallas and one of my cousins, Sister Karen Kudlac, taught in a nearby school. She invited Dad to come visit her classroom to share his war stories, so he and mom made a trip to Dallas. Somehow her students found out about the banquet and took it upon themselves to take up a collection to make a third ticket possible. Joyfully, they handed Dad $265 cash, over half the cost of the coveted ticket.

Upon their return home to Wharton, they shared their wonderful news with the rest of the family. If these students we had never met could give such a nice gift to strangers, couldn't I do something as well?

That was when I decided I could and the next morning, before the sun came up, I started making Rice Krispies treats to take to school to sell for a $1 each to hungry students. I made sure that the squares were large enough that they would entice the students to buy, buy, buy. Within a couple of weeks and dozens and dozens of Krispie treats later, we had enough money and I was well on my way to being part of a celebration to remember. (We were given a few donations for our goal, too.)

The night of the banquet was the night we met a most remarkable lady, survivor Helen Colin and members of her family. When I had gone on the field trip with our students, her portion in the video with survivors stuck with me permanently, especially the story of her mother's last goodbye. Because of her prominence in the video, I was hesitant to invite her to our school for the first time. I thought her chances of actually coming to our school were slim. But she graced us with her presence and did so for many years.

Because of that encounter on the night of the banquet, Mrs. Colin and I forged a strong relationship that goes beyond ordinary acquaintanceships. In our conversations that evening, we realized that my Dad had helped to liberate Dachau, the camp her husband had been confined to. This made our connection to Mrs. Colin even stronger and she tearfully hugged my Dad as her hero. I call her my Jewish mother and she honored me by telling others that I was her adopted Gentile daughter.

My Husband, Gabino (Gabby) Moreno Jr.

When I first met Gabby, he had recently moved to Wharton and was managing the local Perry Brothers store. I had just come from a Women's Aglow retreat and was high on the experience I had just had. I worked for KANI radio and was selling advertising, so that was a convenient excuse for him to get to know this pretty young divorcee. The first time we talked, he asked why I was so happy. I explained I was high on New Wine. Needless to say, that intrigued him and he acted like he knew what I was talking about.

The fact that I had 4 ready-made kids under the age of 6 didn't scare him off. He accepted the challenge and 3 months later, March 8, 1980, we were married. He's the one who introduced me to breakfast tacos. Up until that time, I had never heard of such a thing. He ordered some while we were on our honeymoon in San Antonio. Gabby offered me a taste and I was hooked.

When our son Gabriel was born in 1983, Gabby was in the middle of inventory. After 14 hours of labor, our baby arrived, My sister Frances asked Gabby what time the baby was born. His reply: a dollar forty. We had some rough patches in our lives together. We both went back to school in the late '80's... him to cosmetology at WCJC and me to UH Victoria to become a teacher. After working at Sherrill's Barber Shop for several years, he was able to purchase the business, eventually changing the name to Sherril's Hair Cuts.

He loved cutting hair, loved getting to know his customers, loved all the things that went with the business.

He would tell me about how someone was having a hard time and we needed to pray for them. Many of his customers became like a second family to him. When his health deteriorated due to kidney failure and dialysis, he left a whole slew of friends and customers who kept wishing he could return to cutting hair.

After I started teaching the Holocaust, he learned to love the Jewish people and nation as I do, Holocaust survivor Helen Colin became our adopted Jewish mama. He always wanted to go to Israel but didn't know how that would happen since he was afraid to fly. One of his favorite TV shows was "Discovering the Jewish Jesus" with Rabbi Schneider. He would remind me month after month, "Have you sent my donation to the Jewish Jesus?"

Gabby felt like the Lone Ranger praying for a great revival. He never realized just how many people actually were praying the same thing. He dreamed of building a big church, one that could hold thousands of people. He even dreamed of preaching and spilling the beans on how, when he was dating his wife, she asked if he had good teeth. "Yes, and I can count too!" he said as he kicked his foot and snorted like a horse.

He was generous to a fault. There was a certain beggar man who used to drop by the barber shop in East Gate Plaza on a regular basis. Most people, including me, tried to ignore him, but not Gabby. He would give him a few dollars almost every time and tell him he needed to go to church. And the man did show up... for about 5 minutes at the end of the service, so he could say he had gone there, There were times he gave some money to people walking the streets. I know of at least 3 that he blessed with $100 because he felt that God wanted him to.

After he was life-flighted to St. Luke's on that Saturday evening, May 18, 2019, he confessed to the doctor, and the nurse, that he was afraid. He had many crisis situations during the 2 weeks he was there. I would call or text prayer warriors and within minutes, the crisis was averted. By the time the last one rolled around, he was at peace. My son Gabriel and I and family friend Mike Orr from Tres Dias were with him when he passed from this life into the gates of Heaven. My husband of 39 years was not always a good man, but he died a righteous man. He always said marrying me was the second-best thing he ever did... the first was accepting Jesus Christ as his Lord and Savior. He would want that for each of you as well.

(I thank God for the encouragement that Gabby gave me for compiling this book. In fact, he pestered me for years, telling me, "You need to publish your poems! People need to read them!" He believed in me and helped me to believe in myself. Even though we had our share of problems, he was my best cheerleader. May he rest in peace.)

Momma's Kitchen

Some of my best memories from childhood are memories of Momma's kitchen. Momma expressed herself through the things she did in her kitchen whether it was baking bread, decorating cakes, preparing the family meal, or visiting with a friend. My five brothers and sisters and I received an education through osmosis by living and working her kitchen classroom.

No matter what was going on, we always ended up in the heart of the home - Momma's kitchen. Waking up in the early morning was easy because we followed the wonderful aroma of breakfast to the kitchen. The scent of bacon frying and freshly brewed coffee wafted around the corner and down the hall to the front bedroom that we girls shared. Momma worked miracles of love with flour and yeast, especially in the bread, sweet rolls, and kolaches she baked. Not many days went by that she didn't have fresh bread from the oven.

She won several awards for her kolaches, sweet rolls with a fruit filling. She frequently made a batch for the Knights of Columbus bingo game or to share with a friend. Sometimes her kolaches went to help feed a bereaved family after a death or to congratulate parents on the birth of a new addition.

At Christmastime, Momma baked tea rings for the neighbors. She, my sisters, and I worked in assembly line fashion... rolling out the dough, sprinkling on cinnamon, sugar, and nuts, then rolling it up with the tasty filling securely inside. We then placed the delicious treats on a foil-like tray for the last rising and finally, the baking.

One tray would be baking and another rising, as a third was being prepared. As quickly as they were baked, we would finish each masterpiece... adding icing, colored cherries, and more nuts, Then Mom would send us off with her holiday gifts to give to friends all around the neighborhood.

In the spring and summer, we would sweat profusely in Momma's kitchen as we canned the bounty from the family vegetable garden. As soon as the cucumbers ripened, the pungent aroma of vinegar and dill filled the air. We pickled cucumbers in all kinds of ways- sweet, sour, dill, bread-and-butter, chowchow, hamburger slices... you name it, we made it.

Our family favorites were dill pickles put up in wide mouth Miracle Whip jars. (We were recycling long before it was popular!) We added plenty of garlic and jalapeno slices for extra zest.

When Mom thought we had enough cucumber pickles, she'd have us pickle other vegetables, too, like green beans, okra, and beets. Besides all the pickles, our cupboard was filled with green beans, corn, tomatoes, and a concoction Momma called "soup mix," which was a combination of vegetables for making soup when cooler weather set in.

Momma was the perfect example of the woman who was praised in the last chapter of Proverbs: "She gets up before daylight to prepare food for her family."

Vegetables weren't the only thing we stuffed into jars. When the dewberries were ripe, we'd make beautiful, dark purple jelly. As figs softened on the trees, we'd gather them to make fig preserves. Tangy muscadine grapes provided us with fruit for grape jelly for the coming year.

When autumn winds began to blow, Mom and Dad would be found together in the kitchen making sausage or packaging freshly butchered meat. They usually slaughtered a hog on one of the first cold snaps so we'd be well stocked with bacon, pork chops, ham, and sausage for the winter.

Sometimes Dad would have deer meat to add to the pork to make the sausage leaner. We also butchered beef as well as chickens. We apprentices learned to pluck and clean chickens at a very early age. Although it was unintentional, Momma led many a person into temptation. Every time she cooked with the attic exhaust fan running, passersby would be greeted with the aroma of a juicy roast, zesty sauerkraut, or scrumptious fresh bread.

"Mmmmmm, that sure smells good!" They'd stop and say. Mom often rewarded their compliments with an invitation to join us for supper, or, at the very least, a sample of the goody-of-the-day.

Two things in Momma's kitchen never changed. One was the window above the sink, where we watched nature while washing enough dishes to supply the US Army. I enjoyed the antics of dive-bombing birds or the family dogs giving chase to a squirrel near the pecan trees. Even more fun was squirting my brothers with the spray hose on the kitchen sink as they walked past the window.

The other constant was the old Chambers stove Daddy bought for Momma when they built their home in the late 1940's. A few years ago, Dad thought he'd do Mom a real favor and get her a modern stove. The Chambers was demoted to the garage in the name of progress. Mom tried that newfangled thing and got more frustrated with it each time she cooked on it. It didn't take long to restore the faithful old-timer to its rightful place of duty and honor in the kitchen and banish the new model to a place of shame. (My brother John still uses that Chambers stove.)

All kinds of sounds were an integral part of Momma's kitchen, too. The air was filled with the hum of the Mixmaster, as polkas and waltzes poured forth from the AM radio. There was also much conversation.

Family members prayed before meals, brothers and sisters joked and argued and women shared recipes. Toddlers giggled as they were tickled by their elders, children recited homework passages, parents gave orders, and Dad reminisced about his days in the military during World War II.

Sometimes the conversation was lively as grown-ups held forums over coffee and sweets to discuss the problems of the world. At other times, it was somber as a teenager poured out tales of a broken heart, or we mourned a tragedy that had taken place in someone's life.

Momma's kitchen became a community meeting room, psychiatrist's office, study hall, makeshift dance hall, and even a confessional. Most of all, it was a place of strength and renewal for the members of our family. We all went on to live our own lives, but each of us children took along something we gleaned from Momma's kitchen. My older sister, Frances Pullin, was named the champion kolache baker in Kolache Festivals on several occasions. My younger sister, Helen Monfrey, worked for the Pillsbury company as a chef before her death in 2004, One of my bachelor brothers, Leroy Dettling, became a chef in his own right and served as the driving force for the community

Feast of Sharing for 34 years, doing much of the cooking himself, The other bachelor brother, John Dettling, Jr, is also an excellent cook who loves not only to can, but to bake as well. My older brother, Joe Dettling, became an ag teacher as a result of the rural self-sufficiency he learned from our parents.

As for me, the middle child, I really love to make Kosher dill pickles and bake gifts of homemade food to carry on Momma's example of giving.

Momma's kitchen was the heart of their home for all the years that she and Dad lived there. Poor health caused them to move into an assisted living facility in 2007. In spite of extreme difficulties, they were able to overcome circumstances beyond their control. Mom had a stroke in 1992 when she was 69 years old and it caused her to lose the use of her left arm and side. She learned to use a bread machine for her baking and by letting it start the dough for her, she was able to finish by using her right hand for kneading and shaping into loaves. She made the most of her life until she passed away in June, 2014.

Bread remained one of her specialties and it was always baked in the Chambers oven. With Momma's supervision, Dad learned how to can and he improved his cooking skills as well. He had a reputation for making great pancakes, stupendous coleslaw, and, of course, pickles. Dad lived his life to the fullest until he passed on in February, 2008.

The Book of Ecclesiastes states that there is a time and season for everything. Momma's kitchen was the epitome of that passage. There, we could laugh or cry, tear down or build up, prepare to plant or harvest, mourn or rejoice. We found time to be silent and time to speak and although we had our rivalries, learned to love, too. Dad had known war, so to us the time of peace in Momma's kitchen was precious.

The lessons we learned in that hallowed place included the importance of caring and sharing, hard work and personal responsibility, making do, doing without and improvising. Then there was the greatest lesson of all ~ maintaining a steady faith in the goodness of God.

No matter where we go, we always carry with us the values of love and life that we learned from Mom, Dad, and each other... lessons best remembered from living life in Momma's kitchen.

(This article originally appeared in print in *Country Extra Magazine* in January, 2001. I wrote it to honor the most remarkable woman I have ever know... my mother, Geraldine Wendel Dettling. I can only hope to emulate her tenacity and courage. I love you, Mom. Thank you for the example you set for all of us.)

In Honor of John Dettling, Sr.
11-12-16 to 2-23-08

For once in my life, I'm overwhelmed by all I could say about Dad, but don't have nearly enough time to do so. I guess his war stories would be at the top of the list for memories. We could almost play them in our heads as began each recitation. Out of all the tales he told, the number one tale was how he and his group of men captured over 30 German soldiers as prisoners...

While walking along the hedgerows in France, he and the soldiers with him caught a couple of German soldiers who were out in the open. After they took them into custody, one of the other soldiers wanted to shoot them on the spot. Dad told him that they were not going to kill them and to put his gun away. Then Dad frisked one of the soldiers and found a rosary. He made the sign of the cross and kissed the rosary and gave it back to the soldier.

Dad was fluent in speaking German, and as he gave the rosary back to the soldier, he told him to pray for the war to be over so they all could go home. The soldier was shocked and asked, "You mean you are not going to kill us?" Dad said, "No, we are only doing our job. We want this to be over so we can go home, too." Then the soldier motioned toward the little hill to the soldiers who were hiding there. Within minutes, about 37 soldiers came out from behind the hill. After another unit came to take away the prisoners, Dad and the other American men went to look behind the hill.

They found all kinds of machine guns and ammo set up and ready to shoot. Had they not stayed calm, there would have been a different ending to the story, Another story he frequently told was how he came out of the war with only one broken finger, like the statue of Jesus that he saw in France.

The statue's finger had been damaged in the war, but all that was hurt on Dad was the finger tip of the pointer finger. He always says God protected him from harm because he came home with only his trigger finger needing repair. He could have had it fixed, but he wanted to keep it as a reminder of the faithfulness of God.

Have you ever heard how he paid for the house that he and mom raised us in in Wharton? One day when he cut General Omar Bradley's hair, they talked about the money he was making on the side... General Bradley told Dad that he must be making big money cutting hair, Dad replied that although he was making money, it wasn't doing any good because he wasn't allowed to send it home because of Regulations, The next day, however, Dad received a very special letter... Bradley had written a letter of permission for him to send the money home to his family. Because of that kindness, my mother saved up the money he sent and when he returned to the states, they used it to build the house on South Caney Drive in Wharton that they lived in for over sixty years.

Dad was a character, to put it mildly. Everyone who knew him knew that, but what you may not know is that as long as he was able, he would begin and end his day, kneeling at his bedside to pray. I hardly ever remember him not taking time to ask God's blessing on the meals he ate each day, even in restaurants.

Up until his retirement, we never knew him to take a real vacation. We children longed to know what it was like for a full week family vacation. The closest we ever came to that was a long 3-day week end and, very rarely, 4 days in a row, when a holidayfell on a Saturday or Tuesday. However, he and mom made up the difference after they retired. They were able to travel to many places and he thoroughly enjoyed himself. He especially liked the royal treatment given to them when he and mom visited my sister Helen and her husband Mark in Dallas. In spite of his love of travel, he never had the desire to return to Europe to visit the battlefields that became so much a part of his life.

Dad was an enigma in more ways than one. He was tightfisted when it came to spending his hard-earned money, but he was a horn of plenty when it came to doling out fresh vegetables from his garden. He let people help themselves to his tomatoes, okra and figs, but he made sure that whoever got eggs from him paid their dollar and a quarter because, "the chickens have to pay for their feed."

Up until 2007, Dad loved to dance. He still loved to dance after he and Mom moved into the assisted living facility. My brother John made a u-tube presentation of Dad dancing with the Easter Bunny at the Legacy during the last spring that he was alive. Another of his passions was dominoes, especially 42. Folks at the Legacy (Assisted Living) said having Dad live there really livened things up for everyone. There was rarely a dull moment when he was around.

Even after moving away from their home, Dad's favorite job in the fall was to shell pecans. He kept all members of family supplied with fresh pecans that he shelled religiously after each new crop came in. We could always find him out back behind the house, cracking away.

Even after he and mom moved away from their home, he could still be found on the back porch of the nursing home, shelling those ever-loving pecans.

Dad was dedicated to his God, his family, and his job, whether it was barbering, mowing grass, or serving as a night watchman at the hospital, or even shelling pecans in the fall of the year. He taught us kids and my children, too, his work ethic. He or mom would pick us up from school on Monday afternoons and we would head out to a potato patch, a field of green beans, dewberries in a country pasture, or whatever else was in season. My kids said that he said, "Put your rear up and your head down and start picking!"

His feet weren't very big, but he left shoes that are too big to fill. We're missing him, that's for sure. May he rest in peace till we meet again.

In Honor of Helen
Helen Dettling Monfrey
November 10, 1961 -January 9, 2004

On a Friday morning in January, I watched a flock of geese flying across a clear blue sky. I couldn't help but think of Helen and how she had made her earthly departure that morning, assisted by angels whose wings she had seen the night before. Then I thought of a song that many churches sing with a chorus that says "Some glad morning when this life is over, I'll fly away like a bird from prison bars has flown, I'll fly away."

It was just like Helen to fly away on such a beautiful morning. She loved flying and traveling. When she was growing up, she always said that she would have a job where she could travel, and travel she did. Now Helen has made the ultimate trip with celestial wings of glory.

How do you honor a person like Helen who made such an impact on the lives of people around her? Her presence in life was great, but her courage in facing death was even greater. When the chemo treatments caused her hair to fall out in clumps, she chose to speed up the process by just shaving it all off and displaying her shiny bald head. She really had the will to overcome this thing and chose to live every day to its fullest.

Helen was a powerhouse of sheer will and determination who was just as full of love and a generosity as she was full of stubbornness. She was outspoken throughout all her life but spoke of peace with God and forgiveness to others especially in these last weeks. She loved to have company and thrived on treating each and every visitor in her home and even in her hospital room as special guests. When she couldn't do things for others on her own, she continued to show hospitality above and beyond the call of duty. On my last visit with her, she amazed me by asking if I needed a drink.

We grew up having faith in God and His goodness. That faith sustained Helen through her life, her sickness, and in her passage from this life to the next. After doctors gave her their last prognosis, she told me, "I am dying and I am going to see Jesus."

What a privilege we had to watch her accept this challenge in life with grace, peace, and a calm assurance that God was in control, regardless of the outcome. It was hard on all of us to listen to her plan her own funeral and what foods to serve at the luncheon following the services, She even threatened to come back to make sure it is done right!

How do you honor an enigma like Helen? With praise and admiration and thanksgiving for a life well lived and an unforgettable memory of a wife, a daughter, a sister, an aunt, a cousin, a friend who showed us what it is like to really live. The Book of Revelation in the Bible talks about the marriage feast of the Lamb of God and how grand and glorious that day will be. Maybe God took her early just so she could use her culinary skills to help prepare that greatest meal of all time. It wouldn't surprise me at all to find out she's telling the angels how to set the table and what flowers to use to decorate. All I can say is .... You go, girl! We love you and we will see you soon.

In Honor of Edmunda Wendel
December 28, 1924-April 29, 2001

My mother's younger sister, Edmunda Mary Wendel, was a very special woman, She was named for her Dad, Edmund Joseph Wendel, and she was as unique as her name.

In her younger days, Edmunda served as care giver to many of her nieces and nephews. I suppose she changed more diapers for us than I can count and probably ironed an unknown number of hampers of clothes as well. She was hooked on Jack LaLane and keeping her girlish shape by exercising with him. And she always seemed to have some sort of embroidery project going so she would have a gift to give when weddings and graduations and such took place. She kept that habit up for most of her years in Wharton Manor and left behind a box of thread and a bib waiting to be done.

I remember when she would take care of elderly people either in Wharton or in other locations. Some loved her like a daughter while others took advantage of her simple faith in people. Some called her "Eddie," while others called her "Amanda." There were probably other versions of her name that followed through the years. For most of us, though, she was just sweet, simple "Edmunda."

As I went through her things in Wharton Manor after her death, I found all kinds of hidden treasures and keepsakes. I found quarters from bingo games, trinkets decorating her desk and light fixtures, stuffed toys galore, and numerous little pieces of jewelry and knickknacks. I was especially intrigued by a rather heavy closed shoe box.

As I lifted the lid, I discovered the real threads of her life...pictures, letters, notes, and cards that she had received over the past years from those who loved her and cared for her. What a tapestry she wove into our hearts! This was the grandest embroidery pattern of all, formed by her relationships with friends and family who gave her strength through the ravages of time.

She was indeed one of a kind! I never ceased to be amazed at how she planned her wardrobe... certain colors for certain days, with very little variation until the end. You wouldn't catch her wearing slacks on Sunday! To her that would almost be a sin! But she would wear a pink outfit one day, green another, and blue on another, with maroons sprinkled in from time to time.

She was always excited when I brought her something new to wear and she dutifully oohed and aahed over it, but it always showed up unworn in her closet. When I asked about the lack of use, she gave any one of a litany of excuses... too long, too short, too big, too whatever. The one most original was, "They won't allow me to wear that kind of clothes in here." When I finally got frustrated over the situation, I told her just to tell me if she didn't like my choices so I could take them back to where I bought them. She just gave a sheepish grin and giggled in return.

Other than clothes, it didn't take much to make her happy. One of the greatest treats she looked forward to was the little container of pudding that I brought her from week to week when I brought her laundry to her. Chocolate was her favorite, but she accepted the others almost as eagerly.

If I missed coming personally to get her clothes for a week or two, she smothered me with hugs and kisses when I finally did get to see her again.

Bingo was one of her favorite activities and winning it served a real purpose for her... the quarters she saved up helped her to "pay" for my laundry service or the toothpaste or other things that she wanted.

Yes, Edmunda may be gone physically but the tapestry of her life remains intertwined with ours. I speak from my heart as I relive telling her, "Edmunda, I love you!" and her squeaky echo in reply, "I love you, too".

Lazarus Came Forth

He was just a mongrel puppy, nothing special in any shape, style, or fashion. The tan baby was tiny, and extremely weak from some unknown ailment. Although he was about four weeks old, he didn't even fill two hands when we picked him up. He was so pathetic he couldn't lift his head, much less take nourishment. We never gave him a name, either, because to my way of thinking, we had enough pets already. I did my best to ignore him, thinking he would be dead in just a day or two if he was left alone. But my husband made a statement that I could not ignore... "You need to pray for him."

How dare he tell me to pray for that dog?! With a very stubborn and calloused attitude, I shot back, "And if I pray for him, he's gonna get well and we will have another mouth to feed!" We had 5 kids of our own to take care of and a couple of dogs and cats but little income, so with that snide remark, I thought it was over. However, that was before my conscience kicked in and I knew I needed to talk to the Lord about that little rascal. Proverbs 12:10 (NIV) says, "The righteous care for the needs of their animals, but the kindest acts of the wicked are cruel." I professed to be righteous, so I needed to do my part to care for his needs.

Repentance led the way for me to approach the Throne of God. With a simple prayer and strong belief in the power of the Almighty, I offered these words: "Lord, You see this pup and You know the condition he is in. I ask You in Your mercy to touch him and heal him in Jesus' Name." That was it--- no fanfare, no big fancy words, no display of emotion... just the knowledge that God was in control.

Well, it didn't take long to see God at work. The next day, the pup could lift his head slightly and started drinking milk. He got stronger day by day and, just as I predicted, he did get well. After a few days, my husband asked me, "Well, now that he is better, what are you going to name him?"

Considering the chain of events, the name was obvious. "Lazarus" came forth because of his close call with death, Lazarus grew and became a playful member of the family, with his own cheerful personality. Every time I looked at him, I remembered God's touch on his life and I was humbled to think how close I had come to having my own selfish way. It has been more than 35 years since he was part of our lives, but I will never forget how Lazarus came forth, As he grew, my faith did, too God was able to take care of us, above and beyond what we could imagine.

And if He cared for a dying doggie, how much more did He care for us as His children?

Even the Dogs

"I'm afraid there is nothing we can do to help her. The best we can do is try to help her through the next three weeks till the puppies can eat by themselves. Then we'll decide what to do for her. I'm sorry." The veterinarian shook his head sadly as he gave me the diagnosis.

Noel was the small house dog we inherited a few months earlier from our daughter when she moved out, and less than a week before this doctor visit, she had given birth to a litter of 6 vivacious puppies. But when we returned home after a long day at our jobs, Noel could no longer walk on all four legs. In fact, it was all she could do to drag herself around by moving her two front legs.

We talked about attaching roller wheels under her mid-section and other possible means of mobility, but there seemed to be no solution to the problem. We were stymied as to what might have happened, but we knew this was indeed a serious situation.

X-rays showed two discs in her back had blown out and left her paralyzed from just behind the should blades down. Before the doctor left the room, I questioned, "You mean that short of a miracle, there is nothing we can do?"

"Yes," he replied, "that's right." And he turned to go to his next patient.

A lady came to me immediately after the doctor left the room and asked if I believed in the power of prayer. She caught me off guard and blessed me all at the same time, since I am usually the one asking other people that question.

"Yes, I responded whole heartedly, "I certainly do!" And with that, she and I grabbed hands and laid them on Noel and began praying for healing, in Jesus Name, right there in the waiting room of the veterinary clinic, not caring who was watching or hearing.

We spoke the Word of God as two people gathered in His Name and asked Him for mercy for this animal. We spoke Life, not death, and we reminded Him of promises from the Bible and our right as His children to make this petition, After exchanging names and other information, we went our separate ways and I left in awe of the mysterious ways of our sovereign God. I kept her updated on the healing process as it took place.

For the next few days, Noel tried bravely to care for her pups. She literally pulled herself in and out of her box with them so she could defecate outside of their area. She left long trails of diarrhea feces as she tried to keep her babies clean, I felt so sorry for her as I cleaned her mess, but I realized she was doing her part for healing to take place. Very slowly and surely, she showed signs of improvement.

Her first attempts at standing were wobblier than a newborn colt because she couldn't balance her legs. She walked like a drunk, wavering back and forth and falling down time after time. As time went on, she became steadier and her pups grew strong and healthy because of their mother's love and dedication. Within weeks, she was showing improvement, but unsteadiness gave way to stability and before long, she was running and jumping like nothing had ever happened. And when she was fully healed, she ran figure eights around the yard. Many times, I reminded myself that she was rejoicing in the miracle working power of a loving God.

When I took her in to be spayed after the pups were weaned, I reminded the vet of the problems she had before. He acknowledged that she had indeed had a miracle and that it was only through the goodness of our Creator that she had pulled through. We ended up calling her our "miracle dog" and used her testimony on a regular basis to tell others about Jesus' ability to heal and deliver. The miracle took place in 1995 and Noel, who was already about seven years old at that time, lived about five years longer, and she stayed strong till it was almost the end of her life. She praised God by running figure eights every chance she got and her antics showed just how grateful she was.

Some people might question why God would heal a dog and not people with dreaded diseases. Sometimes that confounds me, too, but then I remember that people can let their own lack of faith interfere with the process. Animals, on the other hand, have a tendency to accept prayers and they want to be restored to health.

The Bible says a righteous man cares for the lives of his animals, (Proverbs 12:10). I suppose that Jesus is the ultimate example of loving and caring for all creatures and great and small. The Bible also says He cares for the lilies of the field and provides food for the birds of the air. (Matthew 6:26-30)

One of the stories about Jesus in the Bible tells how a little Gentile lady asked Jesus for a miracle and told Him that even the dogs get the crumbs from their master's table. (Matthew 15:22-28), I know from experience that He can and does give healing, even to the dogs.

If He cares for the animals of His creation, how much more does He care for you and me? His word is full of promises that areours to claim and profess and obtain healing in our own lives and in the lives of others, Yes, He does care... even for the dogs.

I'm Royalty!

I am the apple of my Father's eye,
He has carved me on the palm of His Hands.
I am clothed in righteousness and I am
Lovely as the Bride of the Lamb.
(refrain)
I'm royalty! I'm royalty!
My Father is the King of Kings!
I'm royalty! I'm royalty!
My brother is the Prince of Peace!!!
(refrain)
I am precious in my Fathers sight,
He knew me before time began.
He knit me together in my mother's womb
And He guides me with the palm of His Hand,
(refrain)
I'll reign with Him for all eternity.
I am holy as the Bride of the Lamb.
In glorified body, I will reign with Him
In the New Jerusalem.
(refrain)

My King My Lord

(Lord, you are so Good to Me)
to be sung to the tune of "Both Sides Now", By Joni Mitchell written by Elizabeth Dettling Moreno, December, 1994

Lord, You are so good to me!

You took my sins, You set me free!

And I'll praise You eternally

For all You've done for me.

You put my feet on solid ground,

You lift me up when I fall down,

You have turned my world around,

And I give You praise.

Refrain

You are my King, You are my Lord,

You answer me before I call.

You extend Your hand to me.

I praise You, Jesus, Lord, my King

Praise and worship, shout out loud!

Hosannas ring beyond the clouds,

Majesty beyond compare,

Oh, Lord, you are so fair!

I sing and dance to glorify
My Father far above the sky.
And as I praise and worship Him,
He sends His peace to me.
(refrain)
Glory, glory to the Lamb,
Who was and is the Great I Am.
Eternal seed of Abraham,
The Father's only Son.
Your Spirit lives within my soul.
Your healing grace has made me
whole. All I have, I give to you.
Your love has made me new.
(refrain)

Catch The Wind

Catch the wind,
The Holy Spirit's blowing through.
Catch the wind!
Let God's Spirit live in you.
Catch the wind!
Let Him blow all chafe away.
Catch the wind!
The Holy Spirit's here today.

Possess the land!
It is ours as we pray.
Possess the land
Our victory will stay.
Possess the land!
With the right hand of the Lord.
Possess the land!
The Holy Bible is our sword.

Now is the time

The Holy Spirit says to come.

Now is the time

Let us gather here as one.

Now is the time

Sing praise to Jesus, our best friend,

Now is the time

To worship God and catch the wind.

(repeat 1st verse)

He Won't Ride a Donkey that Last Ride

Chorus:

Well, He won't ride a donkey that last ride....
He'll be riding a white stallion
When He splits the eastern sky.
And He won't come alone,
Saints will leave their Heavenly Home.
No, He won't ride a donkey that last ride.

When Jesus came before, and He rode into the town,
He rode in on a donkey's foal
that never had been bound.
He was no conquering king
Though the palm leaves they did bring
As they honored Him as He rode along the way.

But people were upset that He was so meek and mild.
Quite often they complained
that He would love a little child.
He did not fit their mold,
Yet He called them to His fold.
They rejected Him and sent him to His death.

But He will soon return, to convict the world of sin.
His armies He'll bring with Him when He comes again.
He will be our conquering King
As the loud Hosannas ring
And we'll reign with Him for all eternity.

Now, my brother, are you ready for that call?
Have you made Jesus your King and Lord of All?
Oh, sister, please don't wait.
He is standing at the gate.
And you alone can choose to let Him in.

Awesome!

Awesome is a word
To describe my Lord;
Holy and righteous is He.
His mercies extend
From the heights of the sky
And down to the depths of the sea.

Awesome is the way
That He cares for me.
He never slumbers or sleeps.
Awesome is protection
That He gives to me
As He defeats all my enemies.

Jesus is the Name
Of my awesome God.
Jehovah Jirah is He.
He created all things in the Universe,
But He still resides within me.
(repeat 1st verse)

Jesus, You're Amazing!

Jesus, You're amazing!
You're holy and You're true.
Jesus, You're amazing.
I submit myself to You.

You're wonderful You're marvelous!
You're mighty God! You're true! Jesus,
You're amazing!
My hope I place in You.

Jesus, You're our Savior.
You came to set us free.
You came down from Heaven,
And You died upon the tree.

You came to Earth; You dwelt with men,
You died to set us free.
Jesus, You're amazing!
Please, come live in me.

Jesus, You are coming
To take Your church away.
You're preparing homes in Heaven
For us for that glorious day.

Forevermore, we'll dwell with You
Throughout eternity.
Jesus, You're amazing!
You share Your life with me.

The Grass Withers

(Isaiah 40:7,8,9,10)
Paraphrased by Elizabeth Dettling Moreno

The grass withers and the flowers fade
But the Word of our God stands forever.
The grass withers and the flowers fade,
But the Word of our God stands forever.

Shout joyfully, oh, shout and sing!
The Lord our God is the coming King!
Shout joyfully, oh, shout and sing!
He rules by His awesome strength.

A Mother's Christmas Story

A little girl asked her mother,
"What does Christmas mean?
I sure do like the presents,
and the toys that Santa brings.
But sometimes I see angels
And a baby and a crib.
I just really want to know,
Is this what Santa did?"
The mother hugged her little girl
And said, "I see I've failed
To tell my precious daughter
Of God's most loving tale."
So she sat down in a nice soft chair
And held her daughter close
And told her the old, old story
Of how Jesus loved us most.

A long time ago in Bethlehem
A lady and a man came into the city,
They were part of God's great plan
The lady's name was Mary,
And Joseph was her spouse.

And that very night they'd add a
A baby to their house.

They traveled late at nighttime,
There were no rooms left for them.
The innkeeper told them they could
stay In the stable near the inn.
There they stayed with cows and sheep
And when their Babe was born,
In the manger He did sleep
On that first Christmas morn.
And angels came from the sky
And sang to shepherd men.
Our Father sent His peace to Earth
On the wings of angel friends.
The shepherds came to visit
And brought some lambs and sheep.
The stars shone brightly in the sky
Proclaiming Godly peace.

He brought the light of Heaven
To live on earthly sod.
The Baby's name was Jesus.
His Father is our God.

He chose to leave His kingdom
So he could dwell with men.
And show His children how to live
With His life and love within.

And so, my little daughter,
Though Santa may seem real,
All the lights and glitter
Are just a lot of frill.
What Christmas means is light and
love That comes from God to men
Our hearts rejoice in Jesus
As we give thanks to Him.

Now, go to sleep, my darling,
And dream of God's sweet love,
And of our Savior Jesus
Who left His home above.
As Christmas comes,
And Christmas goes,
This one truth I know...
Only faith in Jesus
Gives an everlasting glow.

Momma's Easter Story

Written March 8, 1998

My momma says that Easter is a very special day,
Because our Savior Jesus rose up from His grave.
She says that all the rabbits
and the candy and the games
Are nothing that will give us life's eternal gain.
She told me how He suffered and died upon a tree,
Like a lamb, He was slaughtered,
that we might be set free.
She spoke His words of freedom
when He descended into Hell,
Releasing saints from bondage
who've been waiting for a spell.
She almost started crying as she described His
pain and all that He endured to wipe out sin's dark
stain. But then, she started smiling,
because of that third morn,
How His borrowed tomb was empty
after Life became reborn.

And don't you know, with all I've heard,
He's my Savior, true!!!
So if you read the Bible, the story there is clear—
If you don't accept this Savior,
you should tremble with great fear.
Now I know that Jesus IS the MOST important thing, Not of rabbits, toys, or candy, but of Him alone I sing.

Out on the Pier

August 8, 2005

I met with God on the pier today
Early this morning as I went to pray.

I poured out my heart, I bared my soul,
I needed His touch to make me whole.

I told Him my hopes, I revealed my fears,
Then He gently held me and wiped my tears.

I asked forgiveness for stubborn sins,
And begged His Spirit to come fresh again.

He patiently listened to all that I said;
He softly reminded me that's why He bled.

After a while, my cleansing was done.
His mercies came new with the morning sun.

Then, without warning, a dolphin jumped up.
I started to smile from my overflowed cup.

How good is my God! How great is His love!
Thank You, my Father, who reigns from above.

You've given me hope, You've made my heart sing
You are King, You are Lord, and my praises I bring.

Saved from the Clutches of Pharaoh

Saved from the clutches of Pharaoh,
Delivered by the hand of the Lord.
He drowned all the foes that pursued us,
Submerged in the sea by His word.

He let us pass through the waters,
Made walls in the sea left and right.
And after our nation crossed over,
He flushed them out of our sight.

No one is like You, Jehovah.
You alone cause the others to flee.
Oh, merciful Lord, You have saved us;
You've shown Your strength through the sea.

You, Lord, are King forever.
You reign in Your mountain above.
You chose to call us Your people,
You shower our lives with Your love.

Chorus:

You are our God, our Redeemer.

You are glorious and mighty and strong.

You delivered us from all of our enemies.

And we praise you, o God, with our song.

(I wrote this at the request of one of my former principals, Dr. Eright Johnson, so he could turn it into a song for his children's choir. They received one of the top awards in their competition.)

Anniversary Tale
By Elizabeth Dettling Moreno
© July, 1993, revised 2006

Oh, the tales they could tell
As they've traveled down life's trail.
Sixty years or more,
Counting courtship, sixty-four.

Johnny, the red-haired country bumpkin,
Fell for Geraldine, a great looking pumpkin.
A country dance hall was where they first met.
After three introductions, the love bug bit.

She was shy, just sweet sixteen.
He was a talker and loved dancing.
Four years later, they were wed.
Twenty-six was his age, he finally said.

He'd already been drafted and it was true
He left Mississippi so he could say, "I do."
Then he took his new bride to Camp Hood and Paris
So he roughed it a while with his fairest.

Uncle Sam said, "Son, come to Europe with me."
His beloved said, "Honey, I'll wait. You'll see."
But before he left, he was home on leave.
They rejoiced and did not grieve.

After a furlough and lots of lovin,
They now had a little one in the oven.
Nine months later, while he was in France,
Their first child made her grand entrance.

Named after her grandma and Dad's foreign chances,
Her mommy chose to name her Frances.
Letters came and letters went
Back when stamps were just a cent.

John's repertoire of stories grew
About himself and his buddies, too.
Europe, France, and Germany,
And all the places he'd been to see.

Close calls came that might have meant his life,
But God saved him for his beautiful wife.
Meanwhile she carried on as best she could do,
Her heart was broken for her marriage was new.

Days to months and months to years,
The war finally ended amid joyful tears.
Life started over for the family of three
And they sure thanked God for their liberty.

They built a small home on South Caney Drive
And they were so glad to be here and alive.
John worked in a dairy, then as a mechanic.
After Joseph was born, he started to panic.

"How can I do this for all of my life?
I want a good living for my children and wife."
He expressed the thoughts he was harboring,
Then they agreed—John began barbering.

By now little Elizabeth was part of the nest.
Three wonderful kids, they really were blest!
But then something happened in '54...
Leroy was born and now they had four.

"This is it!" they thought, "and now we are ready to
raise up our children and life will be steady."
So Johnny cut hair from Tuesday to Saturday
And rested and gardened on Sunday and Monday.

Geraldine was busy with her four little Dettlings
Cooking and cleaning and raising those siblings.
Later on, in sixty-one, the stork flew again.
Their package this time was a daughter, Helen.

And just when they thought they really were done,
Another surprise-- John, their third son.
Each baby was born on a differing day,
However, no baby was born on a Sunday.

She honored the Lord with what she did best,
With six days of labor and one day of rest.
And when the stork was finally through,
Geraldine started to nursing school.

She worked in the hospital for 10 long years
And raised her family with occasional tears.
Then John changed from one skill to another...
Asa security guard, he protected others.

Working so hard and making a living,
Teaching their kids about loving and giving.
Now, at last, both are retired.
After all their hard work, we're really inspired.

They've overcome difficulties
that caused so much strife
And always kept God as part of their life.
"Sixty-four grand years, so long yet so swift.
This tale was for them a heart written gift.

July 5 1943-July 5, 2006

She Dances in Her Dreams

September 30, 2004

She dances in her dreams,
That's when her body's free.
She moves and glides and swings and sways
She dances in her dreams.

She's on the job again
Dispensing pills and care
With meds in hand and a gentle touch,
She's on the job again.

She's working 'round her home
Not bound by chair or cane.
She sweeps and cleans and cooks and cans.
She's working 'round her home.

At night time, she's made whole.
Her memories travel back
To dance, to work, to walk, to move,
At night time, she's made whole.

How cruel a trick it seemed to be
For the stroke to take its toll.
But her spirit fights and still stays strong.
She dances in her dreams.

(My mom, Geraldine Wendel Dettling, had a massive stroke in March, 1992. It left the left side of her body paralyzed and even though it slowed her down, it did not keep her from living life to the fullest. She passed away at the age of 91 in June, 2014)

The Old Soldier

By Elizabeth Dettling Moreno:
In honor of my Dad, John Dettling, Sr.

The old soldier stands tall,
With the help of his cane,
As taps blows once more
Paying tribute to yet another fallen comrade.
He thinks back on his own life,
Now in the winter of his years,
Wondering why he, of all, has been spared.
Though he fought in the heat of many battles,
D-Day, Bastogne, the Battle of the Bulge,
his biggest injury was a broken finger
and he received a lifetime of memories
that return to haunt him when fever rages.
Oh, yes, he lost much of his hearing
because of the clamor of the guns
and he saw young men fall,
lives cut short because of the ugliness of war.
He wonders about man's inhumanity to man,
the hatred that drives despots to overrule freedom,
the cruelty displayed in prison camps he helped
liberate. Ultimately, he thanks his Creator
for the great mercies shown him,

for the chance for his life to carry on,
to try to bring meaning out of the deaths of the
others. Through his loins, hope sprang forth,
allowing him to father children.
allowing him to help bring goodness into the world.
Through his faith in action, he prays to thank his
Maker for giving him each new day
and for providing food and for meeting all his needs.
He rejoices in life with the wife of his youth,
the woman who has stood by his side
in thought, word, and deed for over 60 years.

And as he faces each new day,
he knows that one day, he will be the one
for whom the taps blow.
He keeps on serving his country
with the pride of a disabled vet.
This old soldier,
this man of strength
is the backbone of our nation.
May we all learn from him
that our purpose in this life
Is to serve our fellow man
And to honor God.
with all the days of our lives.

Give Your Flowers

Give your flowers to the living...
Don't wait for folks to die.
Show your love and compassion
Before their lives pass by.
Give your compliments and praises
While their breath and life is near.
Bring your hugs and warm wishes,
Help shower them with cheer.
Don't take their lives for granted,
It's not what loved ones do.
Take advantage of a reprieve,
It's blessing given few.
Flowers wilt and soon are tossed.
Their memories will just fade.
Time is precious while hearts still beat.
Let virtuous words be said.
Enjoy each day that's given.
It's a flower fresh and sweet,
Filled with goodness, grace, and mercy,
Share God's life with all you meet.

(I wrote this before the death of my younger sister, Helen Dettling Monfrey, who passed away January 9, 2004.)

Night Vision

It must have been late afternoon, but not quite dusk. We were at a building that had lots of glass in the wall and people could easily see through. I was outside of the building and looked to the sky, and there, at a 40-degree angle, was a big, perfectly formed cross, made from the clouds. It did not just look like a cross, it was a cross~-smooth on all the edges, undoubtedly made by God Himself. A crowd of watchers gathered on the east side of the building, pointing and staring at the sight in the brilliant blue sky. Others were looking from inside the building in what appeared to be a waiting room for some sort of business office.

After the original excitement died down a bit, I realized the impact and started going from person to person, saying, "Jesus is coming!!! Are you ready? Would you like for me to pray with you so you are ready?" Just as in real life, some listened and asked for prayer, while others bided their time, ignoring the implications of what was soon to come.

When the praying was done, I lay myself prostrate on the ground, not even thinking about the trouble I would have getting up again. I continued to worship God and intercede for those who chose to delay this important decision for their eternal life.

Yes, I praise God for this night vision, but it is now my responsibility to pass the word on. Some of you undoubtedly are ready and join in my witness. Others will think I'm off on another tangent. But the fact of the matter is still here.... Jesus IS coming. Are you ready?

Are You Ready?

We live in crazy times and it doesn't hurt to be ready...

Many of you will think I'm nuts...others will agree with what I'm writing. Whatever your opinion is, it won't make a difference in what I have to say. Ignore my message if you can, But tuck this information in the back of your mind because you might need it in the not-too-distant future.

I serve a king who actually was born in a barn, I recognize Him as my Lord and Savior and His name is Jesus Christ, the most famous Jew who ever lived. Many churches throughout the world acknowledge His life and eventual return by saying, "Christ has died, Christ has risen, Christ WILL come again." That last line is the one I want to emphasize... He is coming back and not everyone will be ready for His return.

If you have not watched the *Left Behind* movies or read the series, you might want to do that soon. You will at least be aware of what is going on. If you would rather read the scripture for yourself, look in the book of Thessalonians where the writer says he doesn't want us to be ignorant of what will happen. The dead in Christ will rise first, then the other believers will be caught up (raptured) to meet Him in the air.

It's scary to think about all the things that will happen to those who are left behind. You can read the whole scenario in the book of Revelation (also known as the Apocalypse).

If you are one of those, I suggest you find a website with specific instructions for those left behind.

Hopefully it won't be too late to seal your fate for eternity. I have shared with you the truth as Noah did with his neighbors before the flood. May God bless you.

The Smoke Writer in the Sky

I remember that January morning as clearly as if it were yesterday. The cloudless sky was a brilliant blue as the sun rose in the east. Everything in nature seemed almost perfect even though I wasn't... I was a bit nervous... I had a teacher evaluation scheduled for that day. As I made the twenty-five-mile trek from my home in Wharton to work in Bay City, I prayed for favor and for things to go well. Then something caught my eye and got my mind off me. A white line of smoke began developing in the sky to the west and as I watched, the line turned into a perfect circle. "What is this?" I thought as another round formed. Then it dawned on me as brightly as the dawn, "Someone is writing in the sky!"

By the time I reached Magnet, the jet had already made two loops and was working on the third. I was so fascinated by these maneuvers that I used my cell phone to call everyone I could think of to share this experience. But who do you call at 7:15 am without causing alarm or causing trouble? This was too good to keep to myself, but there seemed to be few people that I could tell about this magnificent scene. So, I just smiled all the way to work as the circles continued to develop.

By the time I arrived at my school, there were five of these smoky rings floating gently to the east from the west. But the best part hadn't happened yet. By now, I was more preoccupied with the sky writer than I was with my butterflies over my impending observation, Reluctantly, I headed into the building, hoping that I hadn't let my imagination run wild in my preoccupation with the sky.

I actually did find a few other people who, like me, had witnessed the unusual sight. But the most memorable part was yet to be...

My eyes popped wide open as I took one final look before entering my classroom to prepare for the day. To the east, just above the newly risen sun, was one of the greatest tributes made by man to the Son of God. The first loop had transformed in its journey and had become the biggest and grandest ichthus fish anyone on earth had ever seen! It was almost as if the Lord Himself was speaking peace to my soul, assuring me that no matter how my day went, He would be with me. All my tension drained as I recommitted my life to His never-ending care.

It's been several years now since that strange encounter. Needless to say, I never did find out if that pilot knew that his aerial antics turned into one of the greatest symbols of Christianity known to man. I've often wondered if the pilot was just out having fun or if he was on assignment from an airbase south of here. Whatever the reason, he gave me a morning show I will never forget. Even if I live to be a thousand, I will always remember the smoke writer in the sky.

How Aglow Started in Wharton, Texas

Back in 1977, I learned of a Christian women's organization that I felt would benefit our town. The group was Women's Aglow, and their sole purpose was a soul purpose - to lead women to Jesus, regardless of what religious background they came from, or to minister to them, even if they had no religion at all.

I was determined that someone would take up the cause and Wharton would have a chapter. With great zeal, I went from one Christian lady in leadership to another, but none of them caught the vision. I could not understand how they could ignore such a powerful ministry.

One day in 1978, as my prayer partner Marleah was visiting with me at my little house in the country, I poured out my complaint to her. Being the Godly woman that she was, she confronted me with the challenge.

"Maybe you're the one who's supposed to start it," she said.

"How could God possibly expect me to do it?" I asked. "I'm in a bad marriage with four babies and no contacts and no skills or leadership ability. Surely He doesn't expect someone like me to get it going!"

"Well," she said, "You better think about it before you tell Him 'no'!" When she put it that way, the decision was made for me. I decided I was the one, so like Nehemiah, I made my plans to get the ball rolling.

First of all, I arranged for a group to meet in a local restaurant to lay out the hope that I had. I followed this by saving enough money to place an ad in the local paper, inviting interested women to meet with us for lunch. This gave them a couple of weeks to make their plans to join us. When the day arrived for the first meeting, about seven ladies showed up and committed to share the vision with me. A couple of older women told me that they had been praying for such a ministry for our area. Once more, I saw God's hand working out the impossible details.

The group of us decided to meet once a month to lay groundwork. A few more decided to join with us at future meetings. We chose to make prayer and testimony part of our agenda each time we gathered. Sometime in those early days, I was able to attend my first Women's Aglow retreat in Palestine, Texas, and it was glorious! I returned with ways to fulfill the vision I had been given. Some of the local Aglow leaders from the Houston Chapter got involved and attended our meetings in the early days. With their help and encouragement over the next few months, we were able to get a charter for the Wharton Chapter in less than a year.

Wharton Aglow became a powerful work for the Lord Jesus Christ in the months and years to follow. The local Methodist Church allowed us to use their meeting room each month for several years. Our group was able to minister to dozens, even hundreds, of women who were seeker fellowship and wanted to know Jesus better. Many of them became truly secure in their salvation and like the core group, they were aglow, too.

One day I was in the back of the meeting room, wondering what jewels I would have in my Heavenly crown. I was holding my last baby and bemoaning the fact that I couldn't think of a single person that I had led to the Lord. And then He spoke me in His unmistakable voice.

"Haven't you noticed all the women who have accepted Me because of this Aglow?" He said. "Yes, Sir," I replied. "They are the jewels in your crown!" He assured me.

I wept with joy as He explained my reward.

Wharton Aglow lasted for a season of years, but eventually disbanded. But the residual effect is still being felt, and I am forever grateful that, in spite of a lack of self-confidence, the Lord was able to use a nobody like me to do something big for a Somebody like Him.

My Involvement in the Holocaust Remembrance Association

When I attended the funeral service for Holocaust survivor Helen Colin in July, 2014, I never had any idea that I would meet Rozalie Jerome and that I would be "drafted" to be part of the Crossover Project/Holocaust Remembrance Association based in Kingwood. But Rozalie, a Messianic Jew, took the first step to get to know me by buying a copy of Helen Colin's book from me and found out about my relationship with Mrs. Colin. Then she found out that my Dad, John Dettling Sr., was an American soldier liberator for concentration camps in World War II. The rest is history.

Rozalie called me on the following Sunday morning, supposedly to ask about my children's book, *Sancho the Silly Billy Goat*. That should have taken only a few minutes, but if I remember correctly, she ended up spending at least 45 minutes telling me about her mission to bring reconciliation between Holocaust survivors and their descendants and the remaining Nazi perpetrators and their descendants, as well as liberators and their descendants. Talk about a BIG order!

Rozalie had caught the vision from founder Jobst Bittner while she was on a trip to Germany. When she returned to the States, she was consumed with bringing that project to the USA; she began in her own neighborhood of Kingwood, Texas (northeast Houston). Because of sharing Bittner's vision, the March of Remembrance Texas held its first event in 2012. It has happened faithfully every year since, up until 2020, when the Covid pandemic interfered with group gatherings.

In addition to the March of Remembrance, the Holocaust Remembrance Association is spearheading the Holocaust Garden of Hope in Kingwood (an outdoor interactive educational museum focusing on families and young children for the purpose of motivating people to stand up for what is right in the face of persecution, prejudice, and indifference), as well as several other projects that sensitize hearts to the issues of the Holocaust through education, healing, andreconciliation .

When 2017 rolled around, I was invited to be part of the prayer team in preparation for the March of Remembrance event that year. The following year and in 2019, I was asked to lead the conference prayer calls. was humbled to be asked and complied with a grateful heart. Even when the pandemic changed our plans in 2020, we still prayed for God's intervention in what would end up being a series of 5 programs via the internet over several weeks.

Like so many happenings in my life, I see God's hand is totally in control with all that is going on with the Holocaust Remembrance Association, now known as HRA18. I sincerely thank Rozalie for seeing something in me that I did not see in myself. It is my prayer that the reconciliation that we pray for will flood the world with the shalom of G-d

Afterword

It's hard to believe that most of these writings took place over forty years ago, but it is true. Yes, my first marriage was extremely hard and the only thing that kept me sane was my relationship with the Lord Jesus Christ. As you can see by my writings, I depended upon Him to give me peace and guidance.

I know that God bottled up the prayers that I prayed, especially for my husband. My hope sprang eternal until the very end. When I had to follow through with my unwanted divorce, the judge smiled at me and said, "Your divorce is granted. Now you are a free woman!"

When I left his chambers, I cried as I said to myself... "I don't want to be free!" But even as I went on my way, I knew that God was still in control, and even though I didn't see an answer to my prayers, I didn't despair.

I was a "free woman" for two years. I remarried in March, 1980, and started a new life. It was not a bed of roses, but it wasn't as turbulent as my first marriage. We stayed faithful to each other and our vows and he learned to trust God as I had to help us through our difficulties.

In the late 1980's, we both went back to school... me, to finish a degree to become a teacher and him, to learn to be a hair stylist. We both had new careers and a new start in life.

I taught for twenty-four years and retired just before I turned 65 in 2015. He cut hair until he was forced to retire because of kidney failure in 2014. He passed away on May 31,

2019, just days before his 70" birthday.

During our life together, I continued writing a combination of prayer poems, essays, songs, and other types of remembrances of life. Before my husband's death, I was able to publish several children's books. (This was made possible because I had received an inheritance after my mother's death.) It was also during this time that I was able to help Helen Colin write her autobiography.

Writing always was a very important part of my life. As my readers can tell from my poetry in the '70's, I always was a "wannabe" author.

The words burned within me, begging to be put down on paper, and I complied.

My life's journey has taken twists and turns that I never expected. I participate in the Kroger Grocery Store's Author's program and I've been the top book seller in the Houston area a couple of times. I've been privileged to have a great many book signings in schools, libraries, and other locations, and, of course, Kroger Stores. It's been a tremendous blessing to see tears in someone's eyes as they read the inscriptions I write.

As a result of helping Helen Colin write her autobiography about surviving the Holocaust, I've been asked to be part of the ministry of the Holocaust Remembrance Association. Our goal is to bring reconciliation between Christians and Jews, and, when possible, descendants of perpetrators and victims of the Holocaust.

My children are now grown and have families of their own. Thankfully, they don't have to endure the hardships that we had when they were small. All four of them made contact with their birth father in 2018 after 38 years of not having him in their lives in any shape, form, or fashion and they forgave him for abandoning them.

I also went with them in 2019 to offer my own forgiveness and we have renewed a friendship. In fact, we are better friends now than when we were married. He is now a 78-year-old man who lives alone and doesn't know how he could have been so uncaring back then. He is apologetic for breaking my heart. Although he talks about God, he still hasn't let Him go from his head to his heart. I am still believing God to save him.

A friend of mine declared that I am the "best authorette in the world!" That remains to be seen, but that praise makes me smile. I don't know where this journey will take me, but I trust God as my divine Driver.

2023 update

This book, *Psalms of Motherhood and Other Reflections on Life*, was first published in 2021 and has been used by many people for inspirational reading, devotions, and encouragement, with a few laughs thrown in for good measure. Since that time, the Lord brought a new husband into my life. Randy Tolman and I were married on November 6, 2021, and have been enjoying the many exciting adventures God has provided for our new life together.

www.ingramcontent.com/pod-product-compliance
Lightning Source LLC
Chambersburg PA
CBHW051545010526
44118CB00022B/2581